JOSEPH HO[N]

The Dancing Waiters

SOME COLLECTED TRAVELS

Introduction by James Cameron

THE TRAVEL BOOK CLUB
LONDON : 1976

The Travel Book Club
125 Charing Cross Road
London, WC2H 0EB

This edition by arrangement with
Hamish Hamilton Ltd

Printed and bound in Great Britain by
REDWOOD BURN LIMITED
Trowbridge & Esher

For Christopher

When spring came, even the false spring, there were no problems except where to be happiest. The only thing that could spoil a day was people and if you could keep from making engagements, each day had no limits. People were always the limiters of happiness except for the very few that were as good as spring itself.

Hemingway: A Moveable Feast

Contents

Contents

PART FOUR
EUROPE

PART FIVE
AMERICA

Introduction

BY JAMES CAMERON

If it was Einstein who argued correctly that the spoken radio word is in effect immortal, and continues for ever to speed through space awaiting some sort of misbegotten machinery to retrieve it from limbo, then the record of my first encounter with Joseph Hone is there, whizzing endlessly through the empyrean in all its matchless inconsequence. This is a daunting consideration indeed. The conversation must be a hell of a long way out by now, for it was some years ago. At that time Joseph was a BBC producer, and was invigilating some programme of mine, which must have been of a resounding triviality since neither of us has the least recollection of what it was all about, if indeed it was about anything. Few radio talks were about much in those days, and we were paid accordingly.

By and by the gamekeeper turned poacher, and Joe Hone moved across the board to become himself a broadcaster. Not just a broadcaster either, but in my view, somewhat corrupted by envy, just about *the* broadcaster, at least of his own very special and idiosyncratic *genre*. That is a deplorably pretentious but inescapable word, for which he will forgive me. People like Joseph Hone and I do not claim to have *genres*; we work for a living. I have the impression that Joseph works less hard than I; that is because his end-product seems oddly effortless; professional writers sense these presumptuous advantages. He writes exactly audible words, and sayable words; it is his and our good fortune that they turn out in print to be even better.

Surprisingly few broadcasters have this quality. Another who had it was Peter Duval Smith, an old and firm mutual friend of ours, now untimely dead and lost in Viet Nam. Some time ago Joseph Hone edited a collection of Peter's radio scripts called *Ends of the Earth*, a good title, for which I was privileged to write another such Foreword as this. (I am considering in due season publishing an Anthology Of Forewords, to be entitled:

ix

Always the Bridesmaid.) The context is so similar and the analogy of my two friends so close that I must needs repeat myself, since what I believed to be true of Peter Duval Smith I believe to be equally true of Joseph Hone.

'The broadcast talk in this manner is probably the last form of what was once the Essay—a communication personal and idiosyncratic, informative when information was integral to the style but never instructive, conveying the flavour of the man and that of his subject in that order. Contemporary printed journalism, it seems to me, has almost abandoned interest in this sort of thing.'

However that may be, the radio word endures only when it invades the province of print (except perhaps for Mr. Einstein's space-time jazz, which we can ignore meantime) and not always does it successfully survive that sort of embalmment.

For some reason Joseph Hone's does triumphantly. I say 'for some reason' because it is very difficult to define the quality in this sort of work that makes it read as well as it sounds. Every radio workman knows that this is rather rare. Of course a stylist is a stylist, and Joseph Hone most clearly takes a lot more blood and sweat to the preparation of these scripts than he will probably let on, and any pro can see the polish.

It is not easy to put a name to these things. 'Anecdote' is too trivial, 'reportage' too misleading, 'reminiscence' too ponderous. Those of us who are writers to trade are given to referring to our contributions or columns or stories or whatever they may be as 'pieces'. That is not a bad definition of these cameos of Joe Hone's. They are indeed Pieces—pieces of experience, pieces of a book, pieces of life; none of them is a totality, none of them but starts, and finishes, halfway through an episode of existence that is part of the mosaic of a life. He takes a trip on the Orient Express, because of its literary-romantic associations, but he gets nowhere special, because the Balkans *are* nowhere special, and he is not the first to be disenchanted. If travelling hopefully is better than arriving Joseph Hone is in luck. His is a record of sanguine escapades and journeys to somewhere, someone, something that never quite materializes, or not in the manner any of us expected, but that passage is, at least to me, a record of delight.

Like every writer this century (or so it seems to me, being the great exception) Joseph Hone paddled into the shallow end of life in a Prep School. This would seem to be the most fruitful seedbed of literary horrors since the invention of sex. Even in this teeming scene, however, the little Joseph's establishment appears to have been a place of singular dreadfulness—possibly because it was not English at all, but Irish. It must be appreciated that Joseph is Irish too, which gives him both the right and the ability to be joyfully merciless to those poor souls, the Irish urban Protestants. The famous Prep School is therefore a pushover:

'What gave it its ding-dong lunacy and inspired its petty tyrannies was the unrelenting attempts it made to transplant a specifically English madness—Imperial notions, of class, clubs, good form and so on—into a peculiarly alien, indeed hostile environment. More than any English counterpart, the school was isolated in time and place, administering the last rites of a discredited faith to a tiny and often mistrusted minority, in the midst of a nation that had suffered more than any other from the Imperial cause. . . .'

So there did the young Joseph fardels bear, and grunted and froze under a weary life and learned, as all must learn, What It Was Like Behind The Bicycle Shed.

The story takes off to wilder shores: Egypt, India, Africa. His purpose was rarely the same as was mine when for me too the going was good. I was obliged to seek happenings; Joseph Hone was a one-man happening in himself. And still is, and will be.

Author's Foreword

Travel is a mild form of exile. To move about the world extensively and alone in early maturity, as I did, is to come to feel that such journeyings are essentially a dry run, a preparation for all the more permanent exits that strike one in middle and later life: the loss of parents, wife, home, children and eventual death. All these turmoils seem to me pre-figured by the angry customs man on Newhaven pier, the car crash on the way from the station in Belgrade, a night in the cells at Suez, the maimed and blind at India Gate, the deathly furnaces of Benares.

The more I've travelled, the less I've travelled lightly, and each return has been the sweeter. So that now, in mid-life, I am quite happy to stay at home. Or am I? For travel in the past worked its way insidiously into the home too. I travelled too much, was away too long, so that in the end I played neither home nor away. And the familiar—so often then—soon became a platform or an excuse for another departure. There was for me, I realize now, the lure of exile—the need in these journeyings to pre-figure betrayal and disaster before they actually occurred. I believed in some way that by acting this exile abroad, so I would prevent it ever arising in the reality of home. It was a mistaken belief. Travel remained an isolated, lonely business. And the problems of home were not diminished. The familiar remained as difficult to achieve as the exotic. And soon there was peace with neither, because both could not be lived with simultaneously. At home I longed for the plainslands; in the Empty Quarter I thought of nothing but Chipping Campden. 'How happy could I be with either were other dear charmer away' was not the case here. Both dear charmers were equally necessary to me, but equally exclusive in their demands, and so both were lost. I couldn't have my cake and eat it—and my kind of travelling made that very clear to me. I have some sympathy

now, as I never did before, with the classic stay-at-home who
fears that toothpaste runs out, and wogs begin at Dover. At
least he keeps his home, and I am tempted to think now that my
journeys may not really have been necessary.

In this way, for all that it gives in magic and experience, travel
neither broadens nor narrows the mind, but fragments and
divides it. For me it was a drug like LSD that split up my real
world into a hundred psychedelic colours and shapes that didn't
belong to it: it transformed reality into something bearable
because on the 18th of the month I was taking the train from
Victoria to Sofia to catch the Moscow Express. Once on that
train, three days out, marooned in the white wastes with
Borodin and a samovar, I longed for nothing more than 'Knees
Up Mother Brown' and four pints of bitter in the local. And this
is perhaps one reason why so many travellers pack copies of
pre-war Agatha Christie on long journeys; why *Murder at the
Vicarage* and *The 4.10 from Paddington* are to be found so often
left behind in hotels from Rangoon to Rio: as a lifeline home, a
silken cord which will lead their owners safely back through the
labyrinth, which will be a stay against the divisiveness of travel,
a means of softening the blows of departure and return. It was
not, for example, the Taj Mahal itself that I saw when I got
there but an ivory miniature of the building in a glass sphere,
with water that turned to snow when you shook it, a *jeu
d'esprit* which we had on our mantelpiece at home when I was a
child, next to the French travelling clock, at one end from the
long line of 1940's Christmas cards.

Only in one way has this psychological fragmentation of
travel helped me: in the activity of fiction. Indeed it may have
been why I started writing novels—as the only means available
to me of explaining my irrational sense of exile on landing at
Dieppe, of bringing under control the unnerving shifts of time
between 'now' and 'then' which overcame me after a week in a
new continent, and finally—and most importantly—of making
in fiction some lasting reconciliation between the demands of
adventure and our equal need for sanity; of marrying, if only in
print, 'home' and 'away'. We need sane adventure; we need to
be bonded, yet free. That these irreconcilables are paramount in
our natures is both the tragedy and delight of our lives. And
failing to bring them together in reality, as we must, all we may

do, if we are lucky, is to transfer the effort, making it the central tension which may finally be resolved in art.

More mundanely, travel can become a most mundane thing, as happened with me. A roving journalist is no more, and often a lot less, than any other international businessman: a salesman in letters rather than aspirin. The euphoric effects of travel diminish rapidly in proportion to its frequency, variety and duration—and this is true as much for a writer with his imaginative responses as for the gross industrialist with his armament contracts: a truism, of course, but one which no one who has not travelled widely will ever accept. After the first trip there is no other. Something—not much, but something—dies each time afterwards. That first time was utterly special because one knew nothing and stumbled along blindly, pretending to know everything—like first sex. And the banality never arose then, when you first went away into the world, because banality was the essence of the experience, was sufficient in itself to be completely absorbing and exciting. I remember my first time abroad in Paris. It was a very hot summer evening. I went straight from the station to a large café near the Gare St. Lazare, sat down on the terrace and ordered a pernod. And then I looked around very casually—up at the peeling green slatted shutters on a building opposite, the gaudy art nouveau lettering of an apéritif advertisement on a blank wall, a circular pissoir topped and tailed with heads and legs, the buses swaying past with the passengers clinging on to the wooden rails at the open end, the people next to me speaking such fluent French: and the whole scene was both intensely known, yet unknown. This was the first time in fact; yet somehow I had been here, at this café table, a hundred times before. I was at home, yet I was away. I smoked a gauloise and looked at a girl at another table. She came over later and tried to pick me up. I shook my head sagely. And she said 'Ça va' just as wisely and went away. I sat there for an hour, pretending to read France Soir in the late sunlight, and when I left the waiter said 'Merci' for the 10% (as it was then) that I'd left in the little dimpled plastic saucer. Well, the whole experience—so very ordinary—was utterly engrossing, magic and theatrical for me because it was so ordinary and I could therefore believe myself, for that first hour, to be truly French, to be living in France, to be a fixture in the scene, could see myself God-like in my transformation from a schoolboy in Dublin twenty-four hours before to this seemingly suave and practised boulevardier. It was never like that afterwards. No matter how much the drug was increased or varied, I was never able to call forth so simple, so foolish a response to the world abroad again.

From then on the shadows of experience and repetition lengthened, so that after I became a professional traveller a journey from Cairo to Alexandria on the De Luxe Mail was no more, and no less, interesting than one from Paddington to Kemble Junction. You will say that this is an appallingly world-weary, blasé line for me to take . . . 'Surely, surely—the sights, the excitements of Egypt, the Nile, the steamy acrid smells of Cairo, the soft salt sea breezes of Alex, all the Romance of the Orient. What about all that?' All I can say is that this became true for me. Travel faded. Even the strongest, strangest tastes must pall, from horseradish sauce to the Great Pyramid of Cheops. And you may say that I am the world's worst traveller and had no right to the luck that took me to all the places in this book.

Of course it wasn't luck: it was work. And this particularly is what friends at home do not quite understand. Work seems somehow incompatible with travel to many people. And the job of a roving correspondent seems less like work to them than anything—because it must be so 'interesting', and real work, for the most part, must be boring. I am afraid the stay-at-homes have drunk too much with Lunchtime O'Booze in El Vino's and travelled too widely with Boot between the pages of *Scoop*. The Journalist Abroad has become myth, of course. There he is—weather-beaten, raucous, bloodshot in head and eyes, neck permanently tilted from gripping telephones against his shoulder, holding up bars and girls from Santiago to Sydney, starting revolutions abroad and stopping the presses at home. He is our man—here, there, everywhere: the Life of Riley. I exaggerate. But that the foreign correspondent's life is generally regarded as something of a holiday I don't think can be denied.

The truth, from my own small experience of it, is that these days it is one of the most frustrating, wearying, physically damaging and, for the most part, utterly boring jobs in existence. It is the work *non-pareil*. A typical day-in-the-life-of runs something like this: you arrived in the capital late last night after a twenty-hour flight (which included a six-hour delay, freezing in

Moscow airport) to find the hotel room you booked occupied by four Arab women, heavily veiled, getting a lamb stew up on the bathroom floor. There is a conference of non-aligned nations in the city that week, wives, concubines and children included. You are offered alternative accommodation in the swimming pool changing rooms. After two hours' argument—and finally only because you threaten to 'phone the Minister of Tourism (an old personal friend)—the manager ejects the four Arab ladies who are sent to camp in the pool instead. It turns out they should have been doing this anyway, as they are the cooks and servants of the Sheik's fourth wife and as such do not qualify for a roof over their heads.

Next morning you confirm—with a comforting sense of the familiar if nothing else—a few of the many immutable constants of all hotels in what we are pleased to call the 'less developed world': the telephone *works*, but only very rarely, and with long delay, will it get you through to the person you wish to speak to. It will, almost invariably and with the greatest possible dispatch, connect you to people whom you specifically do *not* wish to speak to: such as the local black market dealer, the signal man in charge of a railway junction in the next state, and the persistent receptionist downstairs who, after many visits now, is still hoping that you may facilitate his entrance to New College, Oxford. For the rest—and this goes without saying—you will find that the water supply has been 'temporarily (i.e. permanently) discontinued', your bedroom windows will not open and your door will not close. As a bonus you will usually discover that the entire staff of the hotel (with the persistent receptionist unfortunately excepted) has gone on strike as from seven o'clock that morning.

An hour later, unshaven and haggard, with the temperature at 110 degrees, you arrive at your first Station of the Cross: the Press Office, hidden behind a mound of sandbags and a platoon of nervous recruits toting very rackety sten guns—sub-standard British army rejects, *circa* 1941, the sort that discharge themselves automatically if the wind changes.

Your old friend Goldfang, the Junior Press Officer, is speaking. He is fat, fiftyish, swarthy, immensely (and falsely) affable, a fund of stories about the time he had last year in the Regent Palace Hotel, has badly discoloured teeth packed tight with gold fillings, and he starts now, as he always does, by threatening in his very bad English to introduce you to his wife that evening. When you get him down to business the Great Equation of all foreign press work quickly emerges. 'You would like to get at something like the truth: we and everyone in our Ministry—and right on up to the Commissioner of Police and the Army High Command if necessary—will devote our best efforts to preventing you getting at it. Furthermore, and as a matter of course, we will diligently lie to you, in the measure of our estimate of your knowledge of local conditions. If neither of these ploys deters you and you seem close to any real scent, we will give you the run around, we will exhaust you. We will set up a dozen appointments for you in one day, spread over four different Ministries in four widely distant parts of the city. You will be unable to refuse any of these appointments for you will not know about them in advance. Each will be made for you by the official you are currently with, and each figure in the chain will be of greater importance, so that you will be led gently upwards, helpless through the boiling day, through all the grades from Information Officer to Cabinet or Prime Minister, or even President. He it is (previously briefed by Goldfang) who will shake your hand benignly in the evening, saying how sorry he is, but he must rush to a meeting and would you make an appointment to see him at the end of the week?

Later Goldfang will 'phone you, prostrate on your hotel bed, suggesting a dinner (with his wife of course) in an interesting little auberge twenty miles up-country. Before you can refuse the 'phone goes dead. On your return to the hotel at two a.m.— stunned from a litre of banana gin, poached python and a near fatal contretemps with a water buffalo on the way back (and now with a very bad go of the squits)—you have at least your marching orders for tomorrow in your pocket: your 'schedule', your 'itinerary' solicitously made out for you by Goldfang's department that afternoon, and discussed with him in terrible detail over the python that evening while his fat wife (or was it really his sister trying to get a U.K. visa?) ogled you. An eight o'clock start with the private secretary to the secretary to the Parliamentary Under Secretary to the Minister of . . . of . . . Of what? 'And where is that Ministry?' 'Well, it's a little way out of town, past the Olympic stadium' (the one they built for the games they didn't get in 1968 and is now almost a ruin) 'then take the Asian highway as far as, as far as . . . well, then you turn right by the big banyan tree and you can't miss it. Then, remember—9.30, back in town. I've fixed you up with . . . And at 10.30 and at 12.00 and . . . Well, it's all fixed, I can assure you.' It certainly is.

This was my pattern of days—for many days, in many places. The only really glamorous thing that ever happened to me abroad was to be the single passenger on a 707 jet from Nairobi to Addis Ababa. I got a lot of champagne and attention. There hadn't been enough room on an earlier flight-load of journalists going off to cover an opening session of the Organization of African Unity and in the vicious squabbling over seats on the apron I'd been left behind, being the most junior and least vociferous of the press corps. As it happened there was this other empty flight going to Addis afterwards in any case. When I got there I walked down the aircraft steps, into the eucalyptus breeze and dazzling sunshine, a splendidly isolated figure with my Olivetti portable and linen tropicals, slightly tipsy, to be greeted effusively and with considerable embarrassment by the Senior Press Officer and many of his staff. Who was this journalist, this mighty man of the pen, whose paper could afford to charter 707s and have their representative travel in them quite alone? Some strange Ju-Ju here and no mistake. Much to the annoyance of my colleagues I was treated officially for the week thereafter with a mystified but intense care, like a Ming vase, suddenly found with a unique pattern on it.

I have talked mostly about the dark side of my travel—the isolation, the boredom. Yet I know as well there was another side to it. I was lucky to travel, and to travel especially in the way I did. I had few deadlines to fill. Once the months of argument and discussion with my employers were over, and agreement had been reached as to what country or continent I should report on, I was usually free to take what angle I choose and, in most cases, to go wherever I wanted. I also had the time, sometimes as long as ten weeks and—most importantly—I had the money: theirs and not mine, and, in the case of the various international organizations for whom I worked, quite a lot of it. On almost every journey too I was independent—quite alone, with tape recorder or typewriter and without any of the impedimenta which make television reporting much more a technical obstacle course than a journalistic one—where the words are tacked on at the end, when you've waited a whole afternoon under the monsoon to get a shot of a prayer wheel in operation.

No, in one way, as with Evelyn Waugh forty years ago, I too can say I travelled 'when the going was good'—going when and where I wanted, ending up saying what I wanted. It is a form of travel now almost extinct. Few people these days can afford the money or the time to travel extensively, outside the package tours, going from one town or country to another almost at whim, travelling first or fifth class, staying at the best or worst hotels, taking life on the run, looking or going or staying at will. It was a gentle perambulation about the world for me, as it used to be with the Victorian travellers, and something which ended on any wide scale in the 'Thirties, in those years before the war when you could spend a month alone, scratching around the Balkans, getting on and off trains at strange stations, looking for Dracula in the Carpathians and living well at the fun for £70. Exactly the same exercise, going by train and staying in average hotels, cost me £590 earlier this year. Yet I could have had ten days skiing in the same area all in for under a £100. But then I don't ski, and don't know that I want to. The plain fact is that to go and do what *you* want abroad these days is a very great luxury. The price of individual travel now is preposterously high, and this should never be. Our spirits have been chained in packages; Prometheus may just manage a week in Benidorm this year.

So if there was boredom, fatigue, frustration in my travel a lot of the time, there was also, underlying this like a soft heart-beat, a euphoric sense of privilege that I was in this strange place at all, that I had got here safely in the first place; that the plane or car or rickshaw hadn't crashed—on my way to Bangkok, to the Taj, to the fiery ghats of Benares; a sense that the mysteries, which most of us have to imagine, were here in front of me, which might not always be there, which I could see and touch and hear before passing on; a feeling of quiet excitement before sleep—even after the most difficult of bureaucratic days—that I had got through the day, missed not one boring appointment, and that tomorrow there would be a whole day free, with no meetings and no talk, when I would be slouched in a train or an aircraft seat looking sleepily out at the Nile or the top of Kilimanjaro, on my way to Kisumu or Cairo: the exhausted being cradled away to the inexhaustible.

The magic of travel, compensation for its sadness, is to feel sometimes, as I did, that one had found the secret at last: an anonymous peace, that one was linked with the world, was part of its wordless sway, was moving unerringly along the right path. In short that one was at home in the place, a globe without exile: in the film of life finally and not, as we mostly are, fighting with the audience, casting ugly shadows on the screen.

I am made aware, on re-reading these pieces, how many of them deal with the British at home and abroad—with a wide spectrum of their experience during the last 150 years, domestically and imperially, from Tunbridge Wells to the wilds of Fort Johnston on Lake Malawi. There were linguistic and other obvious reasons for this: I was working for the BBC, mostly for the old Home Service, and was playing to that market. But I see less obvious and, to me now, uncomfortable reasons for my concentration on this theme.

As I have described here, I was educated, and badly so, in a series of British protestant schools in Ireland. I am Irish. But I have lived in England for the past twenty years, made my life and found my work there. I write this in Ireland shortly after the Birmingham bombings; I live not far from Birmingham; I shall be flying back there next Monday morning. These are the personal, historical and political dilemmas which raise my discomfort, the ghosts of unease.

I have condemned the British in Ireland in these articles. Yet I have praised, by implication at least, the balance of their work and their presence elsewhere in the old Empire. I don't think this inconsistent of me; the inconsistency is true in historical fact: the British have never managed in Ireland. Perhaps like a husband in a bad marriage they have been too close to us, and we to them, for too long. There is nothing left to be said: no room for play, no possible distancing—as there was in Africa, in India and in the Far East, and which enabled the British to leave those places, if with no perfect record, then at least with a small bias of good feeling on both sides.

This being so, why did I, as an Irishman, *choose*—as I certainly did—to concentrate so much here on the manners and mores of the oppressor of my own country?—and why especially having passed through a disastrous expatriate version of their educational system? I believe it was this: that having been a child of disorder, from a broken home, country and school—I longed for order, went to England and found it, first of all personally and after that professionally as a broadcaster, in which job I unconsciously went out to discover and then to map out—for myself more than anyone—the history of that order. I wanted confirmation, in fact, of the intuitons which had taken me from my own country.

The uncomfortable corollary to this is that I, along with many other Irishmeñ, have found in Britain the economic and psychological stability which was not present for us in our own homes —and that having found this, other of our countrymen, with no mandate from us whatsoever, are presently doing their best to destroy that order. I know—and agree with—the larger view here: that England destroyed our nationality over 700 years, and that the millions who left the country were thus forced to leave. This is true historically. But it has not been true in my lifetime. We have been a Republic in all but name for more than fifty years. I didn't leave the history of Ireland; I left the petty inventions of the Free State.

I think that private toleration and public responsibility are the first attributes of the good society; a reflection of my earlier theme here on the individual need for sane adventure. If there is any society which has come close to combining these opposites in its national life, it is the British: sanity in the streets; what you will in your castle. In no country that I have been or lived in is privacy more respected or civic virtue more consistently attempted. Ireland is too flexible, for example—and France the opposite. According to our needs or moods both are marvellous places to visit or to live in. But if it is balance which we want, between the rigid and the lax—if it is opportunity we need to express and to try and reconcile these basic and opposite drives towards freedom and responsibility which each of us must battle with, then we must live in England. For it is a country where the spanking Colonel may readily take the hand of Mrs. Whitehouse. And in such marriage, such astounding compromise, lies the virtue of the place, my reasons for living in it and writing about it. I may not always live in England. But to have done so for as

long as I have is to take wherever one goes a set of happy
standards—a peculiarly English belief in the absolute necessity
of sustaining two quite separate and opposite needs in one's life;
of giving full play, in their season, to madness and concern.

Finally—the sermon ended, the collection taken, these
journeys to many heavens in the world completed—a return to
this haven near Dublin, safe momentarily from the cordite
fumes and disaster, the Jumbos and the motorways, hearing the
endless cry of rooks in the high trees all round the house, watching the rain fall steadily this Sunday, comfortably enclosed in a
room, with the heat on now and the window closed, a room
where all week, the glass wide open in the warmth, I could see
the Wicklow mountains distant and blue in the sunshine, now,
so much more typically, shrouded in rain and cloud, the weather
of a thousand years in this land that makes the moss grow up
your feet as you drown in it—finally, with the renewal of these
familiar whiskey-drinking 'soft days' which will last the rest of
the winter, I know that it has all been worthwhile: that I have
travelled not very hopefully, but that, temporarily at least, I
have arrived; that I have been away and that now I have come
home.

I must thank particularly the BBC for making most of these
journeys possible: and for the longer escapades the United
Nations Development Programme in New York and the World
Bank in Washington. They were all of them careful, and therefore sometimes tiresome, but finally most generous and tolerant
sponsors. Personally I would like to thank Valerie and Ben
Jellett for the great warmth and hospitality of themselves and
their home in Straffan, Co. Kildare, where this book was edited
and generally got together.

Most importantly I would like to thank my wife Jacky for her
unfailing patience, help, domestic ability—and for her letters to
me—during many absences.

December 1974

PART ONE

Autobiography

1

Behind the Bicycle Shed

[July 1972]

Prep schools were built to create stalwart British 'character'. But quite often just the opposite seems to have happened—they have been more successful in producing wounded men: hearty commercial fellows whose laughter is all a pretence; military wallahs whose crackpot campaigns all stem from some ancient torture behind the bicycle shed; emotionally-crippled vicars; and bruised literary gentlemen—who, perhaps, survive the punishment best, since they can flush the venom out of their system into memoirs, farce or fiction. As far as writers go, these cruel little monasteries, together with the public schools, might have been created to ensure the continued vitality of a large part of British letters during the past 150 years. Writers make a world, create lives, largely in default of an affectionate geography in youth, and many books take as their impetus an attempt to clarify devious early experience. Everyone who goes to such schools becomes the young Swann, lying awake, waiting for his mother. And if Proust's book was, in essence, a magnificently sustained fuss over a goodnight kiss, their awful success stems from the same initial dispossession. They are founded on despair and take their shapes and strengths from every kind of refusal. They live on at the head of imperishable memory because the pain was sharp indeed, and they form a natural resource for literature, for no one has written a true book about happiness. What happened behind the bicycle shed or in the headmaster's study creates permanent standards of outrage and disgust: we are rarely so offended in later life.

But was it all really as bad as that? Perhaps the fault may sometimes have been ours in that we were more than usually difficult children? Let us see. Let me state the case. And even though it be for the prosecution, I shall try and be precisely fair. The school was the first of my universities. It was Low Church Protestant in the Arnold tradition of religious enlightenment and physical punishment. Like so many others of its kind, it had been founded in the high noon of Empire, at the turn of the century. It was not a snobbish or particularly expensive school: these were its hopes. It was for a new class that wanted to ape the ways of an old world, and sought its advancement in cricket and *Hymns Ancient and Modern*.

The school building exactly reflected the basic uncertainty of these patterns. It was a large Victorian house that made forceful and grotesque attempts to imitate previous architectural glories —in the Elizabethan, Tudor and Gothic moods. There was false half-timbering, oriel windows in the lavatories, stained-glass in the front rooms, an unnecessary moat round the basement and Neo-Gothic doodles and excrescences in relief wherever the architect's imagination had flagged. Originally it had been in the country, but between the wars a crop of pebble-dash suburbs had grown up round it, so that it was isolated in its ten acres of parkland, behind barbed wire and granite walls: an old, eccentrically-mannered lady who said 'Private' and 'Keep Out'. Oh, that I could have taken her advice. With its sharp roofs, spiky adornments, loud red brick and coloured windows, it had a faintly ecclesiastical, yet not unpleasant air: there was a degree of fantasy about the place, a lightness with the firmness, many trees, exotic shrubs and much grass. Like every such school, it had taken over a private house so that parents could be encouraged in their fatuous belief that little Johnny was not being sent into an institution but was merely moving home. It was typical in everything—except that it was situated in the suburbs of Dublin, not Bagshot or Brighton.

The Irish urban Protestant is among the most conformist of creatures. What gave it its ding-dong lunacy and inspired its petty tyrannies was the unrelenting attempts it made to transplant a specifically English madness—Imperial notions of class, clubs, good form and so on—into a peculiarly alien, indeed hostile environment. More than any English counterpart, the school was isolated in time and place, administering the last rites of a discredited faith to a tiny and often mistrusted minority, in the midst of a nation that had suffered more than any from the Imperial cause. Politics and geography, not Common Entrance, threatened its existence. I think its failures and insults stemmed as much from this embattled view of its function as from its profligate human aberration. Arnold's lofty zeal, together with the whole Protestant-colonial ethic, had come full circle here, and his successors saw themselves in a last battle against the ravening horde. In my time at the school, behind the pleasant bow-windowed façade, the Headmaster and many of the staff had come to an exaggerated belief in the efficacy of prayer and the birch, and in their duty to see that we stood firm to the very last.

I was very young when I went there and at that time, just after the war, it was a popular school, with more than forty boarders and a hundred day boys. The Headmaster was a large, kindly man with thin silver hair, a little jowly. I can't remember him ever saying or doing anything. He seemed merely to preside over the school as an honorary presence, like God. He didn't interfere. And because of this it wasn't a happy place—for the older boys at least, if not for me. I arrived there in the winter term—in my memory of those first two or three years it was always winter there. The heating was non-existent for us boarders—no hot water, nothing—and I was perished with a sort of cold that not only chapped my hands permanently, made my ears blue and nose run like an oil-can, but was like the Lord of the Snows, coming in and making a frozen core inside me that never thawed. I must have been literally numb to the taunts and terrors that come to any new boy, for I can't remember any. My faculties had seized up, a defence mechanism against the chill and the loneliness, for that was the only conscious thought I had then, with my mind running savagely over the unbelievable fact that I was marooned in this hell of utter discomfort, and not at home. I spent all my free time crowding the red-hot stove in the assembly hall, vainly trying to push my way into the circle of larger boys who spat on the throbbing metal at intervals, creating sizzling globules, small explosions of saliva—a performance which I looked on then, not with disgust, but as an envied gesture, symbolic of good fellowship and warmth. All this, I am sure, is quite unexceptional: the isolation, the dirt, the cold of a thousand other prep schools. It was not wished only upon us: the dank, dripping washrooms in the back-yard beyond the changing-rooms, miles away from the dormitories, a place where one skidded about over half a century of congealed human detritus; the yellowed margarine less than a varnish on the curled-up bread; the dried excrement on the open lavatory seats. A child has few standards and can make fewer comparisons. He quickly comes to believe that this is how things are everywhere in the world outside his home. A few years later I realized that the staff lived in quite a different manner, with their own food and bathrooms, and that was the beginning of a cunning and a passion for revolt that formed my real education at school.

At the end of my first year, in the middle of another steel-bound winter, the Headmaster died in his bed one night in the tiny room he had next to our dormitory. It was quite unreal, like the end of a chapter in a child's story. We were told nothing. But we all knew. He had been there, but now, for some almost artistic reason, we should not see him again. There was to be another chapter, with new characters. A new headmaster. We juniors waited expectantly for the story to continue. What followed was a reign of terror that lasted five years—a period in my life which, I think, marked me far more conclusively than any other. It forced my character abruptly and completely into ways I should never naturally have taken. The school became an occupied country: the pupils collaborators, resisters or refugees.

On the surface, the new headmaster appeared no more than a disciplinarian, intent on sharpening things up in a school that had become slightly lax. A school inspector would have commended his scrupulous authority: the purposes of education demanded no less. How, then, could he be guilty? He resorted only to the common violence of such schools: he beat people vigorously, and slowly pulled the hair on the nape of their necks. But that was nothing. Why was it then that in his previous school, as I afterwards learnt, he had been savagely beaten up by some senior boys, trussed in rope, daubed in red paint, bundled into a sack and dumped in the Wicklow Mountains? The reason was simple: the man was a cardinal straight out of the Inquisition. He presented a permanent and awful psychological threat, seen or unseen. He had that rare quality of really sinister omnipresence. He was fearful in his insights and prophecies. In the way of transgression, he knew what you had done, by divination, and exactly what you would do before you did it. He made no formal inquiries into your conduct. He had no need. With him, retribution didn't catch up with you: it never left your side. I remember him once saying to a group of us, caught and about to be beaten: 'Behold, I am with you always, even unto the end of the world.' His gifts were exactly those of a skilled police interrogator who convinces you that your best friend has told all an hour before and that you are there merely to confirm it. He used these methods on the boys—playing them off against each other, placing informers and bribing potential Fifth Columnists—like a master spy running a network. It was a Cold War situation and in those five years I became an adept in all the arts of counterespionage. I do not exaggerate. The school became a foreign country where one had been placed before the war and now moved about, ever alert, in disguise.

He was rather an ordinary-looking man—such men always look rather ordinary—grey-faced and fanatically neat in everything. He would marshal a pin on his desk as if its disruption threatened the balance of the world. He seemed to have been constructed like a piece of machinery, bit by bit, according to some perfect blueprint. It was quite impossible to imagine him naked or washing, or even eating—for he never ate in public and was, in fact, never seen anywhere in the open except on exact business. He knew the importance of withholding himself, knew that the unfamiliar is half the fright in fear. And he wore rubber-soled shoes at a time when that commodity was in very short supply in Europe. I can hear the minute squeaks now as he made his final run-in for you: he had a habit of swooping out of the sun or from the darkness of the laurels down the drive, and taking you like a hawk by the back of your neck.

Most boys gave up any idea of learning, for we lived night and day in fear and enmity. All our behaviour was dictated by the possibility of his sudden presence and fury. We learnt to scan minutely any area of the school before we moved into it, never to sit in a room with only one exit, never to take up any exposed position, never to round a corner, always to have an alibi. To survive was to dissemble, continually and completely. And because of this atmosphere one formed no close friendships in the school—any more than an agent will risk betrayal by making himself known to a colleague. The boys, separated from each other, took comfort in inanimate objects: in the secrets of their lockers and tuck-boxes, and in the forbidden life of the suburban High Street that lay beyond the laurels. This drab thoroughfare of grubby sweetshops, newsagents and greengrocers full of damp cabbages was home to us: a glittering country over the border for which we continually risked everything. It became a matter of honour to creep through the evergreens, usually in the evening, and show ourselves like heroes under the misty street-lamps for a moment, before darting into a shop for some useless article which we carried back as proof of time spent in a free world. Sometimes one or two of the boarders would try and filter into the crowd of day boys who left every afternoon at 3.30. They were like desperate men in a prison break. They knew the risk, for at just that time each day the Headmaster would start to move hungrily around the windows of his study, which gave onto the drive, his gaze like the recurrent beam of light on the barbed wire, searching for just such hapless fools. One could be lucky and get out during an interval in his attention. More often, the attempt ended in a scene with which I have since become familiar in film coverage of the Berlin Wall: a window would fly open with violent shouts, an emissary would be dispatched, and the boys would be frog-marched up the drive again, disappearing into the dark hall.

On one occasion in my last year I went far down the High Street to an isolated kiosk to phone a girl I'd met in the holidays. The box was round a corner, facing a wall, quite off the beaten track. But when I came out, the Headmaster's big black Austin was at the kerb, the engine idling, he and the matron looking at me. He wound down the window and smiled, then turned back again and revved the engine. I thought for a second that he was going to drive away, that he was powerless because we were in the free country beyond the border. Then he opened the door, turned the engine off, got out and sniffed the air, straightening his jacket before coming towards me . . . I survived in that school through enmity, cunning and a natural egoism. I came vehemently to believe in myself and in all the pleasures which lay beyond the walls. I knew in my last years there that the school was nothing but a wretched Toytown, a fabrication of the cruel and stupid, a sad pretence on the edge of the happy reality that lay at the end of the laurels: the world of girls, illicit visits to the big cinemas in town, and meals with friends in grand hotels. Through various happy circumstances, I achieved all these things at that age, in that city. I learnt to trust my own experience rather than that of the pedagogues, seeing clearly how they had

been soured in the fray that was already sweet to me. I faced the
Headmaster with as much pity as fear at the end of term, on my
last evening in the school: I had seen *Odette* at the Adelphi
cinema, with Anna Neagle having her nails pulled out by the
Gestapo, and afterwards had dined with a friend at the
Hibernian. 'You've been drinking,' he said to me quietly, almost
with sadness, as though I had done something which not he but
only some infinitely high authority could now judge and punish.
'Yes,' I said. 'Vouvray. A light cathedral wine, deliciously
pétillant.' True to form to the last, he delayed beating me until
the next morning, just half an hour before I left for ever.

2

Filmbiz

It started in the late 'Forties in my prep school in Dublin, at the little suburban picture-house at the end of the laurel drive. We boarders were allowed to go to the first house there every Saturday night, but only with the Headmaster's approval of the show, and if our conduct during the week merited this glittering reward. This last proviso resulted, with me, in a somewhat curtailed attendance, while the puritan anxieties of our censor meant that half the films anyway were officially banned to all of us: violence of the worst sort was perfectly acceptable, but any kind of love story was right out. We overcame these prohibitions by slipping into the cinema at various odd times during the week —sometimes seeing half the main bill by skipping games on Wednesday, and the rest of it by feigning illness during first prep the next evening. It was a risky business. To be caught was to be gated for the rest of the term. Thus, since I was ten, the cinema has held a special glamour and excitement for me—as much because of my dangerous participation in the séances as for anything I actually saw on the screen. Most exploits in the weekly G-Man gangster serial paled in comparison with the havoc our Headmaster could wreak in his study if he caught you. Once, he took to posting the duty master each evening outside the emergency exit of the cinema—a ploy that was discontinued when one hapless usher was reported by the management for loitering with indecent intent. But gradually I chalked up quite a score of films which appealed to me in deeper ways than just as a proof that I had outwitted authority: James Mason's day-long pursuit, betrayal and inevitable death in *Odd Man Out*, Harry Lime's similar nemesis in *The Third Man*, the doomed nature of happiness in *Brief Encounter*—these themes of trust and consequent disaster at the hands of a vindictive or uncomprehending world seemed highly relevant to my own circumstances in the school. It was a good time for anti-heroes in the cinema, though they were not called that. The morality of these films is ambiguous, but I had no doubts: Holly Martins, in *The Third Man*, should never have killed his best friend in the sewers, and the girl gives him everything he deserves by walking past him in that last long-shot that Greene had such doubts about and Carol Reed was so sure of.

As a result of this potent identification with heroic failure, my ambition at thirteen was to get finished with all schooling as soon as possible and start my real education, which I saw clearly as that of mechanic behind the silver screen. I wonder what it is in early film-experience which makes most adolescents identify with the stars, and only a very few with the director—the real spring behind their fantasies? From the first I was interested in a film's technique: in the dramatic use of camera, lighting, music and silence. I was not so concerned with dialogue or performance. Virtue lay most often in the gaps between the action, in the long-shots, in that last walk into the distance of Vienna's municipal cemetery. I expect I had come to mistrust words as a means of communication, for in my school they had been used only as carriers of dull scholastic twaddle or as a prelude to punishment—never effectively, or affectionately. Like millions of others, I found in films a lot of what I lacked, or thought I lacked, in life: I was different only in wanting to control the manufacture of the drug.

Shortly after I left school I had that 'lucky break' without which, traditionally, one gets nowhere in movies. I fear the tradition is ever valid. John Ford was coming to Ireland to repeat the success of *The Quiet Man* in a trio of films based on similarly 'authentic Irish' material: a rebelly Civil War story, *The Rising of the Moon*, by Lady Gregory, a pastoral tragedy by Frank O'Connor and a farce based on Percy French's famous West Clare Railway. All were scripted by Ford's literary maestro Dudley Nichols, who had done *The Informer* and other classics with him. Ford was coming, the papers said, and would be recruiting Irish artists *and* technicians, for this was to be the start of an Irish film industry. I lost no time in seeking out the Irish producer of the film. He was kindness itself, but said that the actual hiring of people at my level was in the hands of an English production manager arriving later that week, and would I present myself to him at 3.30 that Friday. Already, I was involved in the cloudy, time-wasting hierachies of filmbiz: subtle and long-winded as a Vatican conclave. The production office was in a small mews at the back of the rugby ground in Dublin, and there were fifty or so people crowding it out when I got there. I assumed there was a match on, until I realized that everyone in the alley was as anxious as I to get their hands on that long-shot. Hours later, when I eventually got into the office, I heard that second great axiom of the movies: 'Come back on Monday.' Monday wasn't as bad as Friday, but there were still quite a few hopefuls hammering vainly on the closed door in the twelve-foot wall. I waited at the corner of the mews until they'd finally disappeared, then, in an instant, I shinned up the wall, dropped down into the yard and was in the production office. A group of small, very smart men in blue suits and rimless spectacles were phoning London and Hollywood. They paused in their machinations, brows beetling. 'You said: come back on Monday,' I advised them. They never asked me how I'd got in, nor had they much alternative but to give me a job. I was made third assistant-director to the Master at a salary of £10 a week plus overtime.

At this time—the mid-'Fifties—Ford seemed to have been in the business for ever. His first important film, *The Iron Horse*, dates from the mid-'Twenties, but for ten years before that he'd turned out innumerable two-reelers: Westerns and other frontier films for the most part. He was contemporary with D. W. Griffith, Chaplin, Lillian Gish and Mary Pickford; his films were generally recognized as among the most notable the cinema has produced. Ford was a legend. But in Ireland, as a result of *The Quiet Man* and his Galway ancestry, he was a living god. Ford was deeply fond of Ireland, in a way that only an Irish American can be. His family had been famine exiles, and, quite properly, he regarded the country as his own lost estate, feeling its history of poverty and suffering as a personal affront which he was duty-bound to commemorate in his work whenever possible—particularly in his Irish films. In the land of his fathers, even more than in Hollywood, he was a man not to be crossed, another technician warned me. Being of Protestant extraction—the faith of the oppressor—I should best keep out of his way: advice which seemed to be incompatible with my status as his 'assistant'. But I should not have worried, for, as I discovered very shortly, an assistant director does not look through the camera and discuss the merits of the view with the boss: he is there to keep the rubbernecks at bay and get the boss a cup of tea.

The first location on the O'Connor story, 'The Majesty of the Law', was in and around a little thatched cottage near Oughterard in the middle of Galway—a wild and beautiful landscape. We were up betimes on the first day's shooting: a stunning blue morning in early March, the small hills a patchwork of various peculiarly intense, yet varied, such as one only gets on Atlantic skies away to the west moist with running clouds. The light was peculiarly intense, yet varied, such as one only gets on Atlantic coasts, coming and going in brilliant spurts of colour and sudden shadow—just the sort of mysterious, changeable light for the cameraman to get his lenses on, I thought, and I was surprised later when I found that no filming was done at all under such circumstances: the camera needed a constant, unvarying light as each shot had to 'match' with the next, which might not be taken until a week later. Filming, I soon learnt, was in constant opposition to the natural order of things.

Ford arrived at the head of a big cavalcade of American cars—completely the star of the show, stepping out into what might have been a stage-set for his Irish vision: the lone, traditional turf-cutter's cottage, the green hills of Ireland. He was tall, almost willowy in the English manner, with slacks over legs that were as long and supple as a dancer's. Walking with him didn't result in any vertical movement: he glided along, *High Noon*-fashion, in a white bawneen jacket, yachting pullover, tweed cap, black eye-patch, and with half a wet cigar rolling in his mouth. He must have been in his mid-sixties at the time: his sight not too good, face deeply lined, hands discoloured. But there was an air of concealed alertness about him. His physical approach to anything was direct and full of quiet intent. No gesture was ever aimless or wasted; he constantly handled inanimate objects as if they were alive—small animals in his hands. He surveyed an empty space from his one good eye with a studied amusement or satisfaction, as if his impairment was a special advantage, allowing him to see things hidden to normal vision. He passed through the physical world singling out and naming its virtues, as an archaeologist will detect and unearth a whole civilization beneath a desert. Ford had that gift of making you live every moment of time, of sharing his chosen values.

Of all this, though, I learnt much later. My first day brought other more obvious lessons. Ford, in common with other energetic directors from the old pioneering days such as Howard Hawks had a rough and ready sense of humour, which he often employed for professional purposes—to draw a performance from an awkward actor or 'blood' some junior technician: a sort of locker-room wit intended to break the tension in a situation—not malicious, though often unnerving for the recipients. These little slapstick performances of his occurred quite frequently in the next three months: a play within the play, during which everyone held their breath, for if they did not serve their purpose in promoting smiles, there were usually tears instead. I was the first to inspire one of his show-stopping theatricals. Rain had driven us all into the big marquee for lunch an hour early, and I had taken it upon myself, as assistant to the Master, to remain outside, peering at the bruised sky, waiting for a break in the clouds. When this came, I went into the tent and sidled up behind Ford like a toast-master. He was at the head of the top table, in the middle of a long story about the old IRA: a lord at a feudal banquet, dispensing every sort of largesse to a hundred or so of his minions. At what I—wrongly—took to be a break in the anecdote, I whispered to him: 'It's brightening, sir. I think we can start filming again now.' There was silence. Ford turned and studied me for a moment very seriously. Then he put away his plate and got to his feet. He reached for his cap and started to fiddle with it in a humble way. 'I'm afraid,' he said to the assembly, 'you'll have to leave your dinners. Back to work. My assistant tells me there's been a break in the weather.' Most people had started to move before Ford, with much amusement, sat down again. It was a bad moment. But he had done me a service, as I think he intended to, in tempering my enthusiasm. I was less free with my advice to him afterwards.

You learnt most from Ford not by talking to him, which was nearly always a hair-raising experience, but by watching how he looked at things. For his greatest gift was his ability to narrate visually: to place people unerringly in their landscape, giving them an identity, not through dialogue, which he kept to an irreducible minimum, but by re-creating their emotional history in their traditions, customs, songs and dances, and anything else which displayed their physical link with life. Sometimes, as in Ireland, he got these traditional links wrong through over-emphasis: his truths degenerate into mere folksiness. But in general his vision, from a figure in a sweeping landscape to the mechanics of bridling a horse, is so accurate that you are convinced by an absolutely authentic spirit of place. He has caught the essence, if not always the facts, of the matter. And the strange thing in all this vision was that, latterly, Ford could not see well at all. He never looked through the view-finder, or watched the daily rushes, and he consulted the script once in a blue moon. There is the story of the worried producer who told Ford he was four days behind schedule on a picture—Ford promptly tore a dozen pages out of the script, saying: 'Now I think you'll find we're back on the mark.' Nor was there ever much editing to do after Ford had finished a film—no loose ends for the front office to start monkeying with. For what Ford had long ago learnt to do was to mount the whole film completely in his head, shot by shot, before he started, then link the story closely with the location, and finally have someone come in and photograph the result. Ford, in fact, had no interest in the mechanics of the business. The only piece of film lore I ever heard pass his lips was: 'Everything's all right with a movie as long as the audience aren't conscious of the machine.'

All that spring we filmed throughout the West of Ireland, every week somewhere new: in Galway town and Limerick, at Lough Cutra next to Lady Gregory's home in Coole, and finally at Kilkee, a little Victorian seaside resort on the Atlantic, the terminus for Percy French's famous West Clare Railway. Location shooting is a caravan that packs up each evening when the light goes yellow—the modern version of the old travelling circus, complete with temperamental fat ladies, strong men, performing animals and dangerous high-wire acts—and most of my job as assistant was to keep at bay the crowds who turned up in a frenzy everywhere we filmed. Like a circus, the unit dies each night in a hundred anonymous hotel bedrooms, and has to re-assert its corporate purpose every day anew. There is no continuity, save that which the director cherishes. And sometimes, hanging around in the rain on blank days, one doubted that the co-operative will would ever return to start the beast up again.

Ford would confine himself to his hotel bedroom, incommunicado, with his huge box of Havanas which Ernie O'Malley, an old IRA friend, carried about with him. The producers moaned long distance on the telephone; accountants loomed ominously in the hotel lobby; actors wandered about brokenly, all got up and nowhere to go; the technicians and lower orders played cards and drank stout by the neck behind the mobile generator. The one thing that Ford vehemently prohibited on location was drink: a useful diktat in Ireland as far as the producers were concerned, but which did not go down well with some of the actors. Only one of them, the famous Irish comedian Jimmy O'Dea, ever had the better of Ford over this, in a scene which would have been a pearl in any of his films. O'Dea, a marvellous rubicund little man, hardly five feet tall, a pixie of a fellow, was having a quiet bottle of stout in the back bar of the hotel after his first day's work when Ford—all six foot four of him, glowering badly, cap pulled well down about his ears—surprised him, saying: 'Now Jimmy, let's start off the way we mean to go on. Put that drink down.' O'Dea's nose rose a fraction over the bar as he fed himself more liquid. 'I will not,' he said. 'My time's me own. After business hours.' 'That's enough now, Jimmy. I'll send you back to Dublin.' 'Right you are. Just say the word.' O'Dea held his ground and Ford eventually retired. O'Dea did *not* go back to Dublin *and* had his stout every evening. Ford could be matched, but you had to be Jimmy O'Dea to do it.

The final two weeks' filming in Kilkee were halcyon days. We went out every morning on the narrow-gauge railway, filming along the line—the squat, Puffing Billy engine shrieking and stammering for the last time across half the stony landscape of West Clare, two canary-coloured wooden carriages full of yelling actors, and the guard's van packed with cameras and picnic lunches. At Kilkee there were scenes of slapstick and Irish railway quaintness: porters falling over themselves and farmers' wives losing all their chickens, lovers' tiffs, and a lot of film drinking and 'Are you right there, Michael, are you right?' in the station bar. This sort of blunt, knockabout comedy was very much to Ford's taste, and he filmed it with relish and fluency, like a man interpreting a recurrent happy dream for the fiftieth time.

On the last evening of the film Ford suddenly arrived at the smallest of the Kilkee hotels where the most junior technicians were quartered. We were just starting a chicken dinner, and he asked if he could join us. And then he did an extraordinary thing. He said: 'What about some wine?' 'Red or white?' the waitress asked, thinking her description detailed, and the choice lavish. But Ford seemed to know about wine, and together we went down to the cellars, where we found racks of fine vintages going back many years. In Irish country hotels there used to be an idea that the fresher a wine was the better, like milk, and so this old wine had lain there untouched for decades. I remember we had a Margaux and a Sauterne, '45 and '47 vintage, at the hotel's usual price for red or white wine—ten shillings a bottle. But what I most remember was Ford raising his eye patch in the bad light of the cellar, closely scrutinizing the labels, fingering the old bottles delicately. There was nothing of the wine snob in his gesture: for him, quite simply, these bottles were effective, well-wrought objects, full of old custom, toil and taste, part of a precise landscape. He might just as well have been handling a finely-balanced revolver. And that was what one learnt most from Ford—to forget all the machinery of the cinema, the scripts, the mechanical tricks: the only real trick was to get out into the world and look at things properly and handle them well.

3

Civilizing Mission

[July 1972]

In 1958 I taught for a year in the town of Suez. At the time I wondered about it. And I still do. The school was a long yellow building with a corrugated roof, at the other end of the main street from the hotel. It sat right on the edge of the desert, so that on coming into the town from the Cairo road it loomed up before the other buildings came into sight, like a small fort, an abandoned outpost from *Beau Geste*, with a wall right round it, a tall flag-post and a lifeless flag. It was a dusty, decaying place since the British had left, but friendly with the roars of about a hundred children and a strangely-assorted staff, who saw their work more as a watching brief than as anything to do with education.

Mohammed Fawzi ran the place: 'Fawzi Esquire', as he liked to be addressed. He considered the suffix an important Anglo-Norman title, resting somewhere between plain mister and being a lord—and quite rightly too. Inevitably, he became known to all of us as 'The Squire'. He was from Upper Egypt, a heavy, baboon-like figure of great charm who had been pushed into the job overnight as a result of Eden's miscalculations. It seemed of no importance, least of all to him, that he lacked any academic qualifications for the job—indeed, that he hardly spoke English. Only a few of the staff had degrees—it was difficult to come by suitable teachers outside Cairo at all then—and Fawzi had that real educational qualification: he was a kind man. There were two other Egyptian teachers there who, like me, had been sent down from Cairo—Cassis and Helmi. We three were the 'bachelor teachers', as Fawzi called us, and it made us the butt of a good deal of cackling. We were singled out as special points of interest by the elder girls, who, despite the fact that they were all Egyptian, seemed as English as the proverbial rose. But then for years, until less than a year before, they had shared their

18

desks with the English: the offspring of Canal pilots and oil-men attending what was then the British School in Suez.

'Neither the Arabian quarter, with its seven mosques and unimportant bazaar, nor the European quarter, which contains several buildings and warehouses of considerable size, presents any attraction.' I read out this description of Suez from an old Baedeker I had brought with me. The three of us were sitting one evening, looking out over the Red Sea from rooms Cassis had taken—small, airless but congenial—high above the oily waterway. We talked on for a few minutes, before the landscape darkened and the flat, white and yellow inconsequence of the town disappeared in the blood sunset over the Ataka Mountains to our right. A veneer of rose and purple spread over the town, the desert turned a smoky amethyst, and the water in the bay could, for once, have been the limpid Mediterranean, and not the dull swell of some ashen lake. The shoddy triumphal arch which towered over the cart-track out of town, with its papiermâché rockets, its daubs in Arabic, its hammer and sickle and garbled slogans, now appeared only in silhouette—a graceful thing, devoid of any propaganda, cut out in soft charcoal from the colour beyond. I'd heard about this short, revivifying twilight in the tropics—a moment of mystery, beauty and imagination. The town of Suez needed it more than any.

I lived at the El Nasr Hotel at the end of the main street, where it crossed over the railway and led on downtown to the 'Arabian quarter', the Indian bazaars and the smells. One of half a dozen Europeans left in Suez, I lived in the 'European quarter'. The El Nasr, or 'Victory', Hotel—in honour of the battle a year before. The school was a 'Victory' school as well, but luckily it had originally been called Victoria College, and so no real change had to be made apart from getting rid of all the English staff. I was there because I was Irish—a convenient nationality in that place and time. The hotel was Greek insofar as Mr. Patholaides, its original owner, ran it on behalf of the Government. Whether because of this indignity or by natural inclination, Patholaides lived in a state of continual nerves. He looked like Alfred Hitchcock—his forehead, nose, chin and neck merging together over the run of his face so that it seemed to have no beginning, middle or end. His real character, though, lay in his mouth and teeth, which opened and crunched to create a succession of vigorous shapes and noises—especially when he excited himself, which was often. Then he would clap his tiny hands as well— summoning turbanned slaves from Nubia who would lope out from dark corners, giving him terrified looks as he continued to applaud and babble Arabic, which he spoke hardly at all, though he had been born in Egypt. Clapping hands wasn't a popular mode of command in Egypt just then, which is possibly why Patholaides so frequently exercised the form.

Despite its musty corridors and cubby-holes, the hotel had no history: no potted palms, no sepia-tinted photographs, no memories, no suggestion of Sir Hugh or Colonel William or even Private Paddock—nothing of the forces of a previous law and order who must have used the place when Suez was a garrison town. Though it had been there for half a century, the hotel completely lacked any human imprint. It seemed as if no one had ever really stayed in it. And perhaps this was so. In my year there the only guests were a group of American archaeologists on their way to a dig in Sinai, and Bill, a laconic Texan engaged in building a new oil-refinery outside Suez. The archaeologists, in their hurry to go native, caused a sensation among the Nubian slaves by cooking their own food on primus stoves in their bedrooms, while Bill never caused any sensation, had his food prepared from tins he got from his embassy in Cairo, and went native only to the extent of drinking himself quietly to sleep every evening on Stella beer, an excellent Egyptian soporific. There wasn't a lot to do in Suez. Sometimes, indeed, the beer tended to get out of hand. At week-ends, when we didn't go to Cairo, Helmi, Cassis and I would buy six or a dozen of the dark-green pint bottles, and struggle back to our rooms through the swelter and there, on beds and chairs, slowly gorge on the golden liquid, muttering, becoming clogged with it, before fading, not into drunken sleep, but into a state of isolated consciousness, giving ourselves over to distant memories and distractions, to thoughts of a previously happy life spent in Cairo or Dublin, incredulous at the ill fortune that had brought us to Suez.

Yet I had joined the group of seventeen Irish teachers in Dublin quite without coercion—in fact, on a wave of enthusiasm which had lasted all the way to Cairo Airport. There had been more than fifty of us chosen to teach in these previously British schools in Egypt, but the ranks had thinned dramatically before our departure. The others, on consideration, had found this civilizing mission too unlikely an idea for comfort. But, for us, just the opposite happened. Our appointment that summer gave us all a new impetus. Besides the travel advance made to us, the opportunities which an imminent departure provided of extending our credit in various hostelries landed us in a haze of good intentions all over the city. We felt we had something to celebrate. After all, on the surface, we were going to rescue the English tongue in Egypt. Chaucer's bawdy insights, Donne's studied conceits, Shakespeare's huge music—all that the English with expected perfidy had betrayed, we Irish would resurrect. In fact, though various sorts of ill fortune, quite the reverse occurred.

The first ill fortune was O'Loughley. For some reason I had been responsible for checking our luggage through at Shannon Airport on the way out. I had asked O'Loughley if he had organized his effects the previous night: a rhetorical question, I'd supposed, meant simply as evidence of efficiency and good will, since he'd only brought a large brown-paper parcel with him to the check-in counter. 'I have everything here,' he said. 'All my tings.' The Cork accent was bathed in good humour. He held up the parcel in front of him with both hands, like an offering. 'Everything . . . ?' 'Yes, here.' In Dublin the previous night, at the station and on the train, O'Loughley had played a number of good jokes—almost entirely consequent on a variety of drinks, including a dozen bottles of stout on the journey and an unknown quantity of Jameson Ten Year Old during a delay at Limerick junction—and I thought this latest hurrah with his baggage was simply a result of the overflow, of that heightened, headachy awareness which follows the orange juice and precedes the real midday crunch. For who could travel 3,000 miles for an indefinite stay with only pyjamas and a mac? O'Loughley could, and had. I wondered how soon he had realized he was unlikely to need either garment in the new climate. Probably next morning at Cairo Airport, where he lurched from the plane into a concrete, 100-degree inferno. He tottered about the place, bear-like, somehow very damp-looking, almost steaming, his hair limp and tufty like a new-born child's.

In the Customs shed he became very agitated. 'The lettering,' he said, 'I can't make it out.' He was looking at the notices in

Arabic everywhere. 'The swirls . . . It's all squiggles.' 'It's Arabic. What did you expect?' 'Roman script.' He enunciated the words, slowly, bitterly—as might some pedantic proconsul led hopelessly astray beyond the confines of Empire. 'How will I be able to tell anything here—the gents, drink, the telephone, all the services. I wanted to telephone.' He sank onto a bench as if the intended message would now already be too late. 'The telephones aren't *in* Arabic,' I said. 'Who do you want to phone?' He didn't answer. It may have been to Dublin, to send on some luggage. He had obviously come further from home than he'd bargained for.

Later that day, at the English School in Heliopolis which was to be our temporary billet, we were assigned to posts about the country. I had the misfortune to draw Suez. The school there, unlike the hotel, was full of a buried or disguised past. At the back of Fawzi's study there was the usual portrait-photograph of President Nasser. At the top of the frame I noticed a dull metal plate with an inscription. Months afterwards, during an empty week-end, I took a closer look at this. The writing—and the frame—was upside down. The right way round, it had once held the image of a military figure: 'Major-General Sir Hugh Percival, Commander, Suez and the Canal Zone, 1908–1912'. I eased up a corner of Nasser to see if this Edwardian personage was still there, only to find a grimy photograph of Windsor Castle, supplied by some educational publishers in Fenchurch Street EC3, and dated 1930. Behind that, nothing. The military wallah had disappeared. With these polite overlays of history the frame had come full circle.

In the old days, before Suez, the basement of the school had been used for all those extracurricular activities so dear to British education, those rugged pursuits through which character is supposedly moulded and happiness usually crushed—Scouting, PT, amateur dramatics and so on. In shuttered rooms leading off the central hall were stored the instruments of all this pain, the littered remains of the white man's burden: scouting staffs, punch-bags, dumb-bells, chest-expanders, smashed cricket bats, a number of bruised bowler hats and tattered amateur editions of Ian Hay's play *The Housemaster*. The new regime, not yet aware of these riches beneath them, left the basement area entirely to the shufflings of lame Hamid, the janitor: this was his dark, cool domain, full of brooms and dusters and small coffee cups. Hamid quite took to me—as a happy repetition of the old regime, perhaps—though we could communicate only in monosyllabic English. I must have given him, through our inability to understand each other, a comforting sense of continuity. It was the heat which had first brought me down here when I had a free period or at week-ends. When I opened the door Hamid was nearly always there, like an animal in the darkness, fidgeting with something or other, making coffee—the shaft of blazing light disturbing him for a moment in his nest. I would go into one of the other shuttered rooms off the hallway and root around—moving layers of ancient, bone-dry textbooks, Durrell and Fawdry's *Maths* and Kennedy's *Latin Primer*, mixed up with old Common Entrance exam papers, Union Jacks on tiny sticks and torn photographs of 'The First Eleven—1929', sifting the debris as an archaeologist might the remains of a vanished civilization. From the classrooms overhead the voices droned: children chanting some religious or linguistic formula in Arabic, moving along the paths of another civilization about which I knew nothing.

In one room I found an old film-projector which I got to work. There was, too, a quantity of even older film in rusty cans, supplied many years previously by the British Council. Here were directions from on high, images of the true way of life, celluloid gospels for the infidel. There was an endless documentary on the Three Counties Agricultural Show in what must have been the early 'Thirties: sharp-faced Cotswold farmers in bowlers, and tall county gentlemen in trilbies moving stiffly with shooting-sticks among pigs and cows, prodding them self-consciously, like politicians in a newsreel visiting a depressed area. There was another about 'The British Police', and one on the workings of the Port of London Authority—'Gateway to the Empire'—with a great many shots of Parliament, Big Ben and Tower Bridge. But the bulk of the film consisted of a documentary history of the First World War: an extraordinarily detailed and violent saga, taken by Allied cameramen, made up of yellowing miles of silent, jumpy film. Here was the whole paraphernalia of disaster, without a sound but with a cruel continuity: the laughing faces followed immediately by the ambulance litter; cans of bully-beef being unloaded, and then

stacks of immense howitzer shells; the soaking, dark, stumpy
French landscape and the running men who vanished suddenly
in a huge blot of white smoke. Late into the night, after Hamid
had gone leaving me a last coffee, I would sit up watching this
mute carnage before walking back along the empty main street,
suffused with faint smells after the boiling day, with smoky
foods and dying spices carried on the oven of air from the old
town beyond the railway. There was the bank, with its portico
and other classical pretensions, the Bel Air Hotel from Bournemouth, the Eastern Exchange Telegraph office and the little
Church of England church—all the life-lines of home, posh but
insubstantial now, like a Korda film-set, bathed in the arc of the
moon.

In my time there I learnt far more than my pupils, who never
really took to Shakespeare's huge music or Donne's studied
conceits: the beautiful, archaic language undid them completely.
But I learnt a lot of history in Suez. The place spoke volumes
about King and Country, the temerity of the old British Raj and
their final come-uppance. It was a little living scrapbook of their
confident expansion, their pride, their awful fall. The grubby
town was a warning to all 'civilizing missions' everywhere, even
that of the Irish, who left the country all together at the end of
the school year, badly beaten by the climate and the Stella beer.
Suez marks, too, the final advance of the Israeli legions in 1967,
and may serve as a memorial to their arrogant expansionism, for
they destroyed the town completely. I went back to look at it
just over a year ago. It's interesting to see what a war of attrition
does for a community which one knew intimately: one has a job
making out where the streets were—let alone the pubs and
cinemas and hotels, where I had filled in so many dull hours after
class. The school was gone. It had been hit in one of the first
rocket attacks and was just a stretch of flattened rubble. I
thought of all that old First World War film lost for ever in the
basement, another war of attrition, the men disappearing in
blots of white smoke in a sodden French landscape. History
buries its mistakes and Suez is a great graveyard now.

4

Going Back

[September 1971]

'Come back Paddy Reilly to Ballyjamesduff,
Come home Paddy Reilly to me . . .'

'Come back Paddy Reilly'—one of hundreds of nineteenth-century Irish emigrant songs; born of a lyric people, songs of a green land, sung by any number of forlorn or merry spirits—in small drawing-rooms, saloon bars, at wakes; in Chicago, Australia, Birmingham. The music made for a marvellous few hours in foreign places, capturing exactly the four provinces, the four green fields of Ireland. The melodeons and fiddles and tinkly pianos—they brought a sense of belonging; they brought tears and laughter and fifty pints of porter and fisticuffs as well. But, of course, the singers never went back home—that, or indeed on any other night; they'd no intention. Ireland was to stay exactly as it was in their memories while they, literally, remade the world elsewhere. No emigrant people, I think, have shed so many false tears about their exile, made such good music out of it, so many fine words—take me home again, Kathleen, the wild colonial boy—while barely remembering the words next morning, let alone believing in any of them. You'd think we were driven from Ireland by the Four Horsemen of the Apocalypse—death, famine, pestilence and war. And of course we were. Yet I'm not sure if that's the whole story.

Long before the British or the famine arrived in Ireland we seem to have been talkers and travellers, people with a temperamental itch to tell foreigners their business—to build, discover, to do things anywhere but home: a vain people intent on justifying their vanity. One thinks of the Irish missionaries and navigators of the dark ages, saints and scholars on the early Christian and mediaeval lecture circuit, people wanting to lay down the law anywhere but home. I think the years of British occupation gave us—among many other more painful things—a cast-iron excuse for doing what we've always wanted to do, for

25

fulfilling our real potential—which was to get out of the place and badger or entertain the neighbours.

A great number of Irish people, past and present, in and out of the country, don't really *like* Ireland. And the guilt of this can be measured in the sweetness of the music about those four green fields: the songs are no more than symbolic offerings of homecoming; an actual one-way ticket back would horrify most of us. We've been robbed of our history at home, but we've fulfilled our temperament abroad. Yet, of course, we do go back, now and again: housemaids, property tycoons, professors, priests, doctors, journalists—perversely, like murderers returning to the scene of the crime. Nothing would keep us from that eventual or annual holiday, that trip to the Wexford Festival, to the Dublin Horse Show, or a great slushy, shamrocky evening at Bunratty Castle, or simply to see Auntie May. We nose rather gingerly round the place, frightened of being taken as being either too Irish or too foreign; awkward, in-between people: remembering too well, too carefully, that a half pint of beer is termed a 'glass' in Ireland and that there's really no such thing as a 'large' whiskey. They all are. 'How are you at all?' we may say to an old face at a Dublin street corner. But the 'at all' doesn't seem to sound right now—not easy, not real. We've lost all the habits. So we slink into the airline office to confirm the return booking and wonder what the weather is doing back home. That home in Birmingham or Chicago or Australia. The exile's return is usually far more painful than his departure. In my case, though, it was nothing as dramatic as that when I went back to Ireland this spring. I'd been brought up and educated there, had left in the early-Fifties and had been back to visit many times since. But not to live, to work. And now I thought I'd take a proper and longer look at the country, not so much at its politics or economy, but at the things I'd liked and disliked about it, the friends I'd known, in twenty years living there. Why had I left the place and might I ever go back there? Those were questions too—at the back of my mind, though. I didn't really expect to see them answered.

Nor was it, in any sense, a sentimental journey. I think that's another *canard* about the exile: to leave one's country in the first place is to be all too much the hard-headed realist. Nor did I mean it to be a long, and obviously part guilt-inspired carp against the things I didn't like in Ireland, and which in many cases had got worse since I'd lived there the crass, the ignorant, the arrogant politicians and their colleagues in the church: the Irish ability to despoil both landscape and architecture on a scale I think only paralleled by the burgers of Newark, New Jersey; the uncontrolled eruption of ready cash in the last ten years which is so closely linked with that destruction. Nobody is quicker at chasing a quick buck than the Irish. They did it with picks and shovels once, and now with bulldozers. Well, I've had my carp anyway. In a more sensible light one has to admit that old buildings and litter-free landscapes are things that go with poverty. And one can't wish this on a people for the sake of any number of Palladian mansions and untrammelled vistas. But you can see already, can't you, the priggish, typical attitude of the expatriate: 'As soon as you get a bit of money you go and ruin the place. You were far better off as you were before.'

As I've said, the outsider wants to think of the old homestead, be it Georgian or thatch, exactly as it was. And it isn't, any more. Wealth, or the signs of it, has come to Ireland; it's the most distinctive—and destructive—change in the years since I lived there: a boisterous, almost Latin-American expansiveness much at odds with the staid and graceful Georgian buildings of the cities: a carefree, hooter-full social electricity in the air, reminding one forcibly of the real character differences between the English and the Irish which their one-sided association and shared tongue has subdued for so long.

The Irish, free of England and in the money, have reached a decisive moment. Indeed, they've taken the decision already: the purity of ancient characteristics, of Celtic isolationism, have been thrown to the winds. They are launched on a stream of gliding Mercedes, waving their red bandana-like £100 notes. These are the icons of the new faith and the Irish are rushing to celebrate their conversion. When I got to Dublin I talked to various friends about this Midas touch—to Conor Cruise O'Brien, a Labour M.P. in the Irish Parliament:

'Yes. Of course, first of all as regards the Mercedes, I think you might be a little bit misled by the Mercedes because I think Mercedes are cheaper here than they are in Britain. Certainly there are quite a few around. I haven't seen many £100 notes. I think you must have been moving in very salubrious circles indeed. But certainly, nobody who lives in this society could regard the distribution of wealth as in any sense healthy, and it's not just a question of abstract justice. I'm inclined to think a lot of the exterior signs of wealth that you see around are rather misleading. The country is, of course, certainly better off than it was ten years ago—obviously. Dubliners who have any money like to spend; they're not great savers, as you know yourself. The result is even a mild rise in actual wealth tends to be accompanied by a spending spree. And I think a lot of the people who give signs of outward wealth are in fact in debt. The great bulk of the population are finding it very, very hard indeed to make ends meet. I'm aware of this daily.'

'It's difficult to talk about the environment, about preserving Georgian houses, when one finds—as one does in Dublin and elsewhere in Ireland—many families with literally nowhere to live at all. Yet the two issues are, or should be, quite separate. It's not a question of building new Palladian mansions at the expense of council housing; it's a question of not destroying the Palladian mansion and of destroying the slums. In Ireland there's been a depressing tendency for the government to do just the reverse of this, don't you think?'

'So far, whereas it has made the usual kind of trendy remarks about conservation and the environment which are expected of people concerned with their image these days, they have in fact behaved in a completely *laissez faire* manner. That's to say, if there is quick money to be made, anywhere, about doing anything in this country—that goes. It's more an American than a European fundamental attitude this, and it particularly affects the way Dublin City is being handled—which is disgraceful.'

Before I started off on a journey about Ireland I put this issue of economic prosperity versus the future of the environment to several other friends in Dublin. And I didn't do this just for the sake of making a talking point: economic necessity, in part, was what made me leave Ireland years ago, while the fact that it's one of the last countries in Europe which still has the chance of preserving its amenities almost intact is the main reason why I, among many others, would like to go back there. Again, you can see the awful self-importance of the idea: 'I make my pile elsewhere and want to spend it in peace and quiet back home—undisturbed by the vulgar money-making ecological upsets of my countrymen.' Why shouldn't the Irish—at last—do well at home? And why should I, or anyone else from overseas, think of Ireland as a sort of private demesne? Nonetheless, I have that tendency—and however you look at it, there are two irresistible wills confronting some very movable objects in this equation: the west European urbanite, who has largely destroyed his own towns, wants to get into the country—Ireland, for example, will do very nicely—and in numbers we must inevitably start concreting the grass. The stay-at-home Irish on the other hand, who've had far too much of a poverty stricken, damp country life already, want to get into their fine and relatively unspoilt eighteenth-century towns and must just as surely ruin those in pursuit of supermarkets and a second car. Eventually they too will want to get *back* into their country, as the burgeoning middle class do already in Dublin, having made that city a much less habitable place. So the circle is complete, destructive as a flaming tar barrel rolling over the world. Can the Irish prevent this happening? Almost alone among Europeans they still have the chance of protecting themselves from the smoke, the fumes, the horror. Will they do so? Most people I talked to about this weren't optimistic. They felt that the present economic success was probably illusory while all too obviously the destruction wasn't. Dr. Maurice Craig, an Ulsterman who for seventeen years was with the Historic Buildings Section of the Ministry of Works in London, 'fulfilled a lifetime's ambition', as they say, when he came back to live in Dublin two years ago. Until recently he was in charge of An Taisce, the Irish equivalent of the National Trust, and he is now involved with a government report on the preservation of historic houses in Ireland. I've known him for a good many years. He's one of the foremost architectural historians in these islands, but apart from that he is a walking and witty library of anecdote and hard information on almost every parish and townland in Ireland. No better person to get a briefing from before I set off on my meandering. I asked him if he thought we'd be able to protect ourselves from that apocalyptic tar barrel.

'It will be a very long time, I think, before our seaboard, most of it, will have the terrible things happen to it that have happened, for example, to the south coast of England. But the danger is, of course, that because it is such an empty country still and because it looks on the surface as though everything is alright, that people will not wake up in time. And that we may in fact allow it to be filched away before we realize it. Already certain parts of the western seaboard in Connemara are quite seriously overbuilt in this way, I think.'

So, there was some money at last in Ireland. And with it, a practically untouched landscape, some marvellous houses, marvellous towns—human artefacts still very much an integral and undisturbed part of the view. And over it all, the sense that I might have arrived back home at the very beginning of the end. I took the main road out of Dublin, going south-west towards Limerick, feeling like an insurance assessor on his way to check the valuables. Two things immediately strike one in most Irish landscapes: the view is untutored, completely unmanicured; the land has rarely given itself over to toil and been humanized: it's rough, ragged, wild—that, and what has been cultivated or planned, parklands and such like, have nearly always slipped back into a green and tangly growth: a lurching estate wall, shrouded formal gateway, cracked elm and larch and beyond them ivy-covered pillars, broken masonry.

One often seems to have broken into Sleeping Beauty land in Ireland: a white horse in a field nudging impenetrable briar and beyond it mysterious, spiky chimneys lurking above a steep growth of chestnuts. And to struggle through into this lost time is to find only the chimneys standing like towers in the wreck of the house. And in the long treeless, stony views of the West there is one white cottage five miles away, across a bog, against the pummelled, dripping skies of the Atlantic. No one lives there; that's a foregone conclusion. It is a cliché, I know—this perennial, empty view of Ireland, yet one which, like the pyramids, never ceases to astound. Was this what had to be done, I wondered, efforts made to preserve ruins? Celtic towers, Norman keeps, Georgian mansions or quaint cottages, all of them gone to ruin. Protect them as a memory to make me and the tourists sigh. Wasn't there anything else to be done? Well of course there was. Here was Naas, for example, a typical small Irish town thirty miles south of Dublin which I'd passed through hundreds of times before and never really noticed. But Maurice Craig had.

'I would like to see the thing rather more in perspective and

not to think too much about great country houses, although we
have some great country houses of considerable importance and
some which are not particularly large but which are also of
great architectural quality, but I'd like to see the quality of our
country towns, for example, more recognized than it is. People
have been going round saying parrot-wise for a very long time
that Irish towns are not pretty like English towns, or Irish
villages are not pretty. To say this is, I think, to miss the point
completely: in the first place Irish villages are not villages in the
sense that English villages are, they are not pretty, they are
beautiful very often, which is very much more significant.
They're sometimes rather severe, they're often spacially very
grand and very splendid. You must remember that the Irish
town had its origin really as a cattle fair, that is why you have
these enormous wide streets in so many of them—great big
streets in a town like Ballymahon or Templemore. They were
improved and tidied up by landlords in the eighteenth century;
they very often have good public building in a commanding
situation, a court house, a market house or something like that.
Very often the churches, the Catholic and Protestant churches,
are placed in a significant relationship to the plan and the whole
thing is really rather grand. And their qualities are only now
beginning to be recognized—just in time because they are under
very serious threat from this mania for modernization.'

That evening I stopped in a small white-washed village in the
wilds of County Limerick. There was the usual late nineteenth-
century grocery cum pub at the crossroads—Murphy's, Keoghs,
Hannigans, you never see a 'Dog and Duck' or 'George and
Dragon' in Ireland. There were some fine gilded mirrors promoting long vanished tonic waters in the back quarter, solid benches
and stools, a pine counter and ceiling that had gone black with
the years; a smell of malt, plug tobacco, a modest girlie calendar
from a firm of bottlers in Dublin, a box for Lepers in the Congo
and a television set with half a dozen old men pondering it.

At the front in the provision store the smell was of paraffin
and bread and there was a marvellous bank of mahogany tea
drawers with brass handles behind the counter. The place was
well kept, a family concern, nothing special about it. I'd been in
such pubs time out of number in Ireland and never thought
twice of it. There was nothing to think about. They were neither

unsuitably old or new, unnecessarily dirty or clean. They were as much a part of place as a muslin-windowed, aspidistrad French provincial café—a Café de la Gare—buildings as perfectly adapted to the sensible Irish trait of conducting business and pleasure concurrently as a French café is to serving drinks on the run. Yet I was going to have to think about these snug and useful Irish retreats from now on. Maurice Craig told me that one of them undergoes the horrific mutation into concrete and formica almost every day now in Ireland.

'It's a race between the growth of consciousness and the speed of dereliction—the movement to preserve some Irish pubs in their quality and the rush to modernize, which has already destroyed so many. It's a question of who gets there first. If we can persuade—when I say we, I mean the sort of people who value these things—persuade a particular public house owner that his public house is really more worth keeping than it is worth modernizing, we may be able to do so in time before he has taken the irrecoverable step, or we may not.'

I went back into the liquid inner reaches of the grocery and watched the box. The six o'clock news was coming on and the old men were all lined up in front of it like greyhounds waiting for the traps to open. The country Irish, at least, take their news very seriously, like Alvar Liddell in 1940. The first item in most Irish news bulletins is usually about the Italian Pope, or preferably about one of his Irish Cardinals, Bishops or Parish Priests, though these days Belfast tends to usurp this holy writ. But tonight something quite different was featured, a topic which ten years ago in the Republic, had you even thought about it, would have guaranteed you a long session in the fiery furnace: contraception. Nowadays in Ireland the topic is barely enough to make your ears burn. Yet, as one might have expected, we've managed to give an interesting twist to the issue. A Bill had been proposed in the Irish Parliament to amend the present law which makes it a criminal offence to possess, and therefore presumably to use, any form of contraceptive. Apparently, as far as the men are concerned, it's not a question of the criminal negligence of having unwanted or uncared for children, it's a matter of changing the law so that they may keep out of jail for an indulgence which few of them seem to care much for anyway. But perhaps I'm being cynical. The issue was raised in any case, and very expectedly in the Irish context, by a woman M.P. who is also a doctor. The old men in the back bar weathered the news of this possible sexual liberation dubiously. They lowered their stout a fraction quicker and passed no remarks. The news continued with an earthquake somewhere, thousands dead, scenes of carnage and desolation. 'Terrible how thin the earth do be in parts' one of the statues said, livening up considerably, on firmer ground now. The Secular State—that's one of the great issues in Ireland now and I suppose in that cause, as everywhere else, we must exchange the old pubs for contraceptive slot machines. The idea of having both might strike us as too much of a good thing altogether.

For as long as I have been conscious of Ireland, in Ireland, going back thirty years, the issues seem to have remained constant; the sulky land, rock-headed politicians, a frozen church, the wound of emigration: a country of ditches, purpose built for lovers, so that priests with sticks could beat them out of it and on to the Mail boat. This has seemed the awful natural order of life in Ireland and one can only be thankful that at last the equation is being queried vehemently. A pub, after all, new or old, need not be the whole of life.

'Bang, bang—lie down, you're dead!!' *Gunsmoke* had come on behind me on the box. The old men hitched their pants up about them, sadly, vicariously, and I went out into the mild and empty evening of the street—that frequent weather in Ireland, unpeopled and deceptive, which suggests there's never been a hand raised in anger in these parts, let alone a battle between young and old, against church or state. And yet one knows that the moral history of the land is made up of just these things. Behind the soft weather, the nice turn of phrase, the bland and sensible newsreader, there has always been the ambush of the old—the bitter, the disappointed, the powerful, the enmity of fools. As W. B. Yeats wrote of the downfall of Parnell:

> 'The Bishops and the Party
> That tragic story made,
> A husband that had sold his wife
> And after that betrayed;
> But stories that live longest
> Are sung above the glass,

And Parnell loved his country,
And Parnell loved his lass.'

A typical Irish drinking song that. Conor Cruise O'Brien had
brought this issue up to date for me before I'd left Dublin.

'I don't want to be glib about it, but the essential thing in this
country is that young people should be able to stay at home in
it, if they want to, particularly in the western part of the country. In much of the countryside there's an excessive proportion
of elderly, rather frightened people, which gives a rather bad
tone to society. In particular, for example, this encourages the
type of politician who is good at trading on the fears of elderly,
frightened people. The problem is of how to keep people at home.
On the current controversy about contraception, the *Sunday
Independent*, which I think has the biggest circulation paper in
the country, has taken a very forthright position in favour of
amending the law. I think all this is to the good. I think in the
nature of things the younger side of this controversy cannot fail
to win. It's a question of how long it takes them to do it. I think
that when the opponents of the change in the law are forced to
bring out their arguments they are bound to wilt in the public
air. Because it's not the kind of argument that really stands up.
For example, in the evening paper today a priest is arguing that
if contraceptives are freely available it will mean that people
will be able to sin with impunity, meaning that the good man
regards a child as an instrument of punishment, which I think
is a fairly dark thought.'

I drove up into the slanting sun along the twisting hill roads
between Limerick and Galway—waves of yellow-flecked gorse
on one side, high up; valleys of bog and stone rolling down to the
Atlantic on the other, the petrified land of the west; no real
grazing anywhere apart from the borders of the road and here
were cows and donkeys and strayed bewildered horses, carved
dead still in the middle of the road, backs against the wind,
forgotten statuary. Dark thoughts. The Bishops and the Party,
Parnell . . . Parnell had lime thrown in his face in Kilkenny
where I grew up, really worse than the usual tactics—a bullet in
the back or a bash from a crozier; the 'Playboy' riots at the
Abbey theatre, O'Casey's exile, Joyce's; the gentlemen of Easter,
1916—who few Irish people cared a damn about until they were

put up against a wall and shot—that heartrending scuffle in which 150 people took on an empire, through which Ireland became free and lost most of her democrats: Dr. Noel Browne and his twenty-year-dead national health scheme. And the rest of us, important only in our numbers, singing those sad songs in Birmingham and Perth: poverty, dissension, betrayal, ignorance, exile, the 'old sow that eats her farrow' ...

This burden of Irish history is inescapable when you go back there, so that one knows partly that one has left the place mainly in order to forget it all. And one can well understand the great cry in Ireland now 'let's forget the past, 1916 and all that, let's get to grips with some kind of future.' But what kind of future? Perversely, perhaps, one suspects it will be cast in concrete and aluminium, a future which will cast us all in the same mode. The late Sir Tyrone Guthrie, who I talked to towards the end of my journey, 150 miles north:

'Do you know what I think? I think there's an awful lot of vain nonsense talked about the Irish this and the Irish that. Look at modern Ireland and the Irish are exactly like the English, exactly like the New Zealanders, the Americans, the Luxemburgers, anybody else. They want to live in comfortable little suburban houses with amenities and their taste is no worse—but no better—than that of any other community. It is perfectly true that Ireland has produced a considerable number of men of genius, largely witty and theatrical genius, but this does not mean, I think, that the average Irishman is wittier or more theatrical or has better taste or anything else than the average person anywhere. He tends to be educated below the average.'

'But isn't it a pity that everybody should end up exactly like each other?'

'But we *don't* end up exactly like each other. Fundamentally we all really long for the same thing. We're all lazy, we like to be comfortable, we want to be thought respectable and we want to be like each other. Look at you and I sitting here in our conventional clothes with our ties.'

'Well I'm in conventional clothes but I'd hardly describe yours as such.'

'I shall be *very* conventional when I leave after lunch to fulfil an engagement. You wouldn't know me from any stockbroker.'

I stopped in Gort for the night, a small market town twenty

miles south of Galway. Lady Gregory's Gort, with Coole Park two miles away, epicentre of the Irish literary revival. Here was one lady who rigorously, vehemently stayed at home and there were two others several counties north, the Gore-Booth daughters, Constance and Eva Gore-Booth of Lissadell House in Sligo. They stayed their ground too. What happened to them and their houses? What was the connection between their Ireland only forty years ago and the one now? Was there a link at all? Perhaps you'll say I was looking for trouble.

I drove up the rutted mile-long drive to Coole next morning. The Forestry Commission run the estate now, the seven woods have become a hundred. A walk leads down to the lake and the famous swans are still there—nine and twenty I counted that morning. Yeats made it nine and fifty—poetic licence perhaps or extremely good sight. There was biscuit paper and orange peel all along the shoreline. They are going to open up the lake drive properly this year—the famous autograph tree in the walled garden has a ten-foot cage round it now in readiness. But it's too late, too many Kilroys have been here already. Shaw's bold flourish remains, but Yeats and Synge are barely decipherable. And of the house itself—nothing. Like an archaeologist looking for a Roman villa one would have to dig for evidence that it ever existed. And this in fact is what's happening now, another marvellously late Irish gesture, the foundations are being displayed in trenches along the grass, showing the original plan, the two bow windows looking west, the porch and kitchen door. I found part of an old telephone in the disturbed rubble, a bell and a tiny rusted hammer. I asked Sir Tyrone Guthrie whether he thought that these historic houses had been let go by the authorities because in some ways they represented the life and manners of the oppressor.

'I would think that was perhaps almost too obvious and melodramatic an explanation—and doesn't hold water at all in the case of Coole or of Lissadel, which were not held by oppressors, but by people to whom the Irish Free State has great reason to be grateful. But I don't think that the Irish Free State as a whole feels grateful, not out of malice, but out of ignorance. I don't think most citizens would have the least knowledge of who Lady Gregory, for instance, or Eva Gore Booth were, or that their contribution to Irish life was in any sense important. I think this is a question of education. And I think in most of the European countries this kind of preservation of the past is a work which has been voluntarily undertaken by the upper classes, by educated and predominantly wealthy people. Well, Ireland more or less dispensed with its upper classes in 1922. There was no regulation which forbad them, but the Government of the State predominantly fell into the hands of lower middle-class people of fairly limited education. And I don't think in political circles in general you would find that there was any strong feeling of the importance of a historical background, the importance to the country of the preservation of houses like Coole and Lissadell. Now it's arguable—I'm not saying that we're right in thinking that it's important, and they're wrong. I do think they're wrong, but I can see that they're not unreasonable.'

The poet W. B. Yeats, on the other hand, has been better remembered in the area. The Norman keep, Thoor Ballylee which he bought in 1919, a few miles away from Coole Park, has been nicely restored from the ruin with cows in it, which it was ten years ago. And a lot of Sligo, further north, where he spent his youth, is now known as The Yeats Country—and there are bars called 'The Yeats Lounge' and 'The Poets Rest', though Yeats must have been unique amongst Irish writers in apparently having been in a bar only once in his life. Nonetheless a prophet was being honoured in his own county, by his own neighbours, even if they were a bit late, and the reasons were financial as much as literary. I talked to the very agreeable Mayor of Sligo that evening, Councillor Higgins.

'Well, indeed it would be true to say that all of us in Sligo, our societies and local authorities, have been very, very slow indeed to see the potential involved in tourism generally. It is true to say we were a little bit late in the field: in, shall we say, cashing in on the great name of the Yeats family generally here in this area.'

This attention to W. B. Yeats is the exception, not the rule. Ten miles west of the town, beyond Rosses Point, along the rim of Sligo Bay, in the remnants of a forest, is Lissadell House, a huge slate-grey, limestone block, rather like a classic mid-Victorian railway terminus in the middle of nowhere. It was the home of Yeats' close friends in youth, the Gore-Booth sisters, Constance and Eva, renowned for their beauty and spirit—two

women whose childhood and subsequent bitter careers Yeats
often returned to in his verse. Constance Markieviez, as she
afterwards became, was among the leaders of the 1916 rising.
Only her sex saved her from execution with the others. Lissadell
House is now occupied by her two nieces, and is badly in need of
repair: strange fate for the home of an almost contemporary Irish
heroine. But as I said before being prepared to lay down your life
for your country doesn't necessarily mean much in Ireland—or
anywhere else for that matter I suppose—not until you're
actually shot. Even today the only official honour which the
Irish Government can bestow on one of its citizens is a State
funeral.

Thirty years ago Lissadell was a huge estate employing more
than a hundred people, rich in mature timber. But there have
been tortuous legal problems since, endless disputations with the
State. Death duties and much else besides. As a result the trees
have been felled and no one seems to know where the money has
gone. The present two sisters live in a few rooms of the huge
house. The rest of the building, echoing and rather damp, is now
open to visitors—though again there was a long legal struggle
to allow that.

From Sligo I drove eastwards, through the wild and little
known mountains between Leitrim and Monaghan, skirting the
border with Northern Ireland at one point, just before Clones—
actually going over into the land of red pillar and telephone
boxes, and out again, a typically Irish no man's land without
customs posts on the main road. What have great houses to do
with Ireland now, you may well ask, in a place full of Mercedes
on the one side and murder on the other? Tyrone Guthrie had
one answer when I spoke to him at Annamakerrig, his own
family house in County Monaghan, a large, long, winding early
nineteenth-century house overlooking forest-crowded hills and
one of the many beautiful lakes of that remote area.

'We're still here because we're very fond of the place. It has
all sorts of associations for us. And we like being here. And I
think it is important, if you can, to have associations with the
locality, and if possible some kind of an attachment to some part
of the world that you regard as home. I think there's a very
great danger, in cities particularly and in the modern economy,
of more and more people becoming virtually rootless. You see

this in America. Whereas if you've been in a locality, as we have here, for quite a number of generations, you grow up with the neighbours. The old neighbours now are my contemporaries. I knew their parents, they knew mine. I know their children and their grandchildren.'

'You've never felt of the place then here as a burden?'

'No, I've never felt that. I do find it expensive. But I'd rather be spending the money this way than going to the races.'

'Do you think that having this house in the background of your professional life—which of course has been led nearly always overseas—do you think this has helped your professional life, in the sense that at the back of you there was this house?'

'Joe, I couldn't answer that. I simply don't know. I think it has helped me. It's given me a feeling of continuity and that I'm working for something rather—as I think—more important than just getting on, or making money. If we had children it would be easy to understand, but since we haven't and whatever has gone on here will end with us, well, then perhaps it is all rather sentimental and irrational.'

Back to Dublin, then, through the throes of spring. And when I got there the city was empty over the Easter week-end. From where I was staying in Fitzwilliam Square I looked down the half mile of soft red-brick Georgian buildings to the bottom of Merrion Street: not a car or a person between the wide cliffs, the tall windows. After ten minutes or so two nuns crossed the road in the far distance, shoes cracking the silence like small pistols going off in an ocean—black and white exclamation marks in the rose sunlight. In the opposite direction the Dublin mountains twenty minutes away. The best equipped, most gracious village in the world. And now it seems as if it was trying hard to be like any other ruined city.

The Irish want conspicuous consumption while the consumptives want Ireland—that Ireland, still empty and easy, the best clinic in the world for the urban cure, and the two factions, I think, can only be on a collision course. As for us the expatriates, we'll keep on coming back every so often and muttering. I suppose we see and feel our Ireland in memory, far too intensely for there to be much comfort in a return to the new Ireland. It's an ungenerous emotion, I know. We're annoyed by our guilt, so that we become ashamed of our love. We're involved in that useless arid dilemma of loving and hating, that twisted mood which brings the passionate songs from all sides of the world in words which we don't really mean at all.

On Easter Monday, I walked down the deserted Dublin quays, passed Gandon's gleaming Customs House, and put my foot up on a bollard. Raw black sewage was erupting on the surface of the water just beneath me, minute depth charges, bubbles of stink, mushrooming up through the brine. And I thought, if those gobbets and globules one day come up to make the whole stream and the roads become one long trail of metal bullets, if the rest of the great houses fall, if that tar barrel concretes all the land and Dublin becomes like Birmingham, you'll have me to blame, and all the other Paddy Reillys, as much as anyone.

Gulls hawked around the masts and funnels of the port, swearing over the water, big as albatrosses, talking with the boats of tides journeys, to Liverpool and Holyhead. I'd come back and now I wanted to go home.

PART TWO

Asia

1

Sunny Dacca

[June 1970]

'I'm looking forward to Dacca,' the man from Chicago said as
we flew up from Bangkok.

'You know it then?' I said.

'No. Never been there. But my wife's joining me. The office
agreed to fly her out. Sort of half-way point. These trips—they
go on so long, God damn it.'

'Where are you staying?'

Al looked at me in astonishment. 'There's only one hotel in
Dacca,' he said. And he gave me the name. Of course. I'd forgotten. The agency in Bangkok had mentioned it and I'd said: all
right. But I'd no idea its services were unique. Dacca is the
capital of East Pakistan, the other half of the country, north of
Burma, in what used to be East Bengal before partition. A confusing place, certainly, but the idea of its having just this one
hotel struck me as no more than a piece of clever promotion on
the part of some Madison Avenue executive employed by this
immense chain of hotels.

I'm fairly used to airport scrambles in what are known, to my
mind often ambiguously, as the 'underdeveloped' countries, but
the touting, begging, cursing and screaming which greeted our
emergence into the forecourt of Dacca airport was incomparable.
A wave of vicious taxi-drivers surged towards us, kicking the
beggars-on-trolleys out of their way, giving them, in fact, a head
start so that these maimed unfortunates made for us like the
start of a go-kart race. Tiny children with huge eyes and hardly
clothes or flesh were as thick as pebbles on the ground, spinning
forward between everyone's feet, so that Al had come a cropper
and lost a carton of cigarettes before we were all escorted into
the hotel limousine like train robbers on their way to the local
assizes.

Al's face sank as we looked out on the passing scene on the
way into town. He was horrified. 'My goodness me,' he said, in

43

what I supposed was a parody of the Peter Sellers record—his only point of contact perhaps with the Indian sub-continent. And indeed one might, I think, without ambiguity, have described the view as 'underdeveloped'. Or rather it was typical of the sort of development which the West has imposed over the years on most of the urban East. The road, the whole landscape, was as flat and characterless and depressing as the sum total of all airport roads everywhere. But as well, it was poverty-stricken —literally. A plague land in mud and corrugated iron. Ferocious pot-holes and a cynically optimistic population count were the most obvious impressions. It was Ramadan and people were hawking vigorously in the gutters, following the Prophet implicitly in not allowing even their own saliva to break their daylight fast. It was a cliché of despair: basement department, lower depths.

Then an immense white building, a splendid example of late Hilton-Moorish, reared up in front of us through the clutter of huts and kerosene flares. In its imposition over the city it would have disgraced any hostelry of the same sort in New York or London. The hall porter, magnificently Hollywood-mogul, bowed us into the suddenly crisp atmosphere and I fancied I could still hear the shrieks from the street. But I couldn't. It was the sound of exotic birds crying in a golden cage by the window, the music of water on marble and 'I can't give you anything but love' from a crooner in the cocktail bar. Al gasped with pleasure and said would I have a drink with him and his wife before supper. 'Put some champagne on ice,' he said, 'now that we're home and dry.'

We very nearly were dry too. The champagne was £20 and I settled for a bottle of local beer at 28s. 6d. instead. Al never turned up. Later I heard someone talking about an American who'd been locked in his room by mistake with his wife, incarcerated. It may have been true: locksmiths and carpenters were going past my room most of the night. The service was impeccable and I'm sure Al was perfectly happy. The rooms were splendid. There wasn't a single thing in them which could possibly have reminded him of Dacca, of Pakistan, of anywhere except America. The pandemonium outside might have been drifting up from 42nd Street. Besides, it wasn't only Al who went to ground: in the four days I was in the hotel no one seemed to leave the place at all. They arrived all right, by the score, unsteady but grateful, like the survivors of some frightful accident: a convention dealing with the problems of the Third World, a Japanese TV crew, German salesmen, UN officials and men from the Chase Manhattan Bank. And within moments, as long as it took to unpack their talcum and after-shave, they'd recovered. After all, the hotel had everything—from 'US-flown T-bone steaks' (£4) to 'country-fresh eggs any style' (7s.). And if you didn't step into an inch of pile everywhere you went you thought you'd broken your ankle. The fairly beautiful people streamed around the shopping concourse on the ground floor— the beauty salons, the gift shops and airline offices—chatting and laughing, sticking close to the lift banks and intuitively avoiding the area round the swing-doors, as though a sudden drop in the air-conditioning might drag them screaming into the real weather outside. No one ever called for a taxi, or stood on the steps of the hotel, as visitors do, taking the air of a strange city. No one talked about the wonderful snaps they'd taken that day; the quaint things they'd seen. No one talked about Dacca at all. The crooner in the bar sang 'I can't give you anything but love' and the girls by the pool had Bloody Marys at £1 a time before the 'Continental supper'. And someone wondered what had happened to his call to New York.

Outside, at many arms' length from the B-movie hall porter, beyond the stunted hedge—the taxi-drivers, the touts, the go-kart beggars and the children waited. You could see them in the evening caught in the blaze of light from the foyer, like a group in a UNICEF Christmas card. Outside, the battlefield, the 'Third World War' as the president of the convention probably summed it all up in the Orchid Room that evening. And really, it wasn't entirely his fault. This, after all, was the only hotel in town.

There was—expectedly—trouble when I was in Dacca last year: language trouble, religious trouble and political trouble, not to mention the go-kart beggars and the others—the trouble of simply surviving in a country which has almost the lowest per capita income anywhere in the world. Provinces wanted the voting and other municipal lists in their own dialects, the Moslems were getting on less well than ever with the Hindus left over from partition with India. But above all the East Pakistanis thought that the larger part of their country, 1,000 miles

away across India, was prospering at their expense. Jute is
Pakistan's major export, East Pakistan produces two-thirds of it,
and the money from this wasn't finding its way back to the
eastern province. As a result of all this buses and cars were being
overturned, shops and houses smashed and burnt, and people
walloped into their graves as a matter of everyday life. And
when one ventured out of the hotel in the morning the roads
were like the remnants of a brick factory and glass crackled
underfoot like puddles after a hard frost.

I thought I'd try and skip the air-conditioning and revolution
—there was nothing much I could do about either—and see
something of the country, or rather, at that time of year, see
something of the extraordinary network of waterways, which is
what most of East Pakistan is during and after the monsoon:
5,000 miles of navigable waters—rivers, canals, inlets and tidal
reaches—an immense flooded landscape in one of the largest and
most fascinating deltaic areas in the world. East Pakistan forms
the basin for three huge rivers—the Ganges, the Brahmaputra
and the Meghna, which after the monsoon turn the country into
a huge bath, with odd sandbanks, palm trees and banana
plantations sticking up here and there—something, one imagines,
like Egypt in the days before the original Aswan Dam.

The hotel didn't seem to offer much in the way of trips about
this liquid world so I went instead to the headquarters of the
Inland Waterways Transport Authority. A retired naval man—
Commander Bajwa—was in charge of things and we talked about
possible trips, poring over maps and schedules for an hour or
two, considering seasonal shifts in the channels and the position
of flood beacons, before he decided I'd never make it on my own
and put himself and the Authority's flagship at my disposal for
the day.

The World Bank has recently underwritten a vast scheme for
improving these essential waterways, so the flagship itself was
something rather smart: a 45-foot, 120-horsepower diesel cruiser
in black and white with honey-coloured teak fittings, a sun deck
aft and a mass of echo-sounding and mapping equipment forward. It was an extraordinary journey, this, pushing gently off
the pier at Narayanganj below Dacca and into the oily stream
with its huge jute warehouses on either bank, like an industrial
canal in the Midlands, and then on past crumbling, crowded

bathing ghats. Extraordinary because, not living on a river or in a country dominated by one, it was easy to be surprised by the fantastic activity on and beside the water: life in East Pakistan is the water. The land is merely a bed to sleep on. There was a film I remember seeing years ago, *The River* made by Jean Renoir, in which everything, even the most stable parts of the plot, was activated by the water, and I thought at the time there must have been a good deal of artistic licence in Renoir's handling of the story. I was wrong: the river *was* where everything happened, the motive behind all psychological and physical movement, for this was the same river—the Ganges—and the film had been made here in what was then East Bengal over twenty years ago.

Soon the channel opened out and the green banks flattened away for miles on either side of us, the sun high and the air suddenly sharp. A line of crumbling battlements and towers and blue-flecked cupolas shimmered on the horizon and I thought I'd seen a mirage at last. But it was one of the several ancient capitals of the province, now, like the others, overcome by shifting sands and waters. In front of this, a line of a dozen men, bent double, hauling a cable, came into sight. They walked like dreamers, methodically, in exact step with each other though yards separated them on the line. Hauling what? There was nothing in sight except a dhow with flaming ochre sails a mile away. They were hauling that: a square-rigged boat, like a Roman war-galley, with a black hull, curved, beak-like prow and a staring yellow eye on either side of it. And inside, when it came towards us, I could see two rows of men below on the half-deck, rowing with huge oars, the rhythm kept exactly with some kind of wooden gong, the blades dipping in and out with short, sharp thrusts, just like the war-galleys in the Battle of Actium in *Cleopatra*. It was a jute boat making its way laboriously up the current to the warehouses.

And then I saw a hundred such boats dotted right down the horizon, each one built and coloured with a subtle difference, all of them spread down the water like caravels at sea in old maps of the world. These were 'country boats'—square-rigged mostly, made of bamboo, of anything between three and 100 tons—and there are something like 300,000 of them in use today in East Pakistan. One-man enterprises giving employment to 300,000

families, so that one didn't need to ask why they didn't have
engines fitted: a quarter of the labour force in the country would
be out of a job if they did. These families take turns in either
pulling or rowing the boat upstream and then collapse on the
journey homewards down the current. The boats hardly moved
against the flow in what now seemed an open sea, with only a
tiny margin of sand a mile away on one side—an armada of toy
ships from a Roman history book, splashes of rust and ink and
half-moons of white sail in a world where there was no telling
between sky and water, which was now everywhere a faint blue.

An hour of this, in a deck chair under the awning with sandwiches and a bottle of 28s. 6d. beer, and I was nearly asleep:
until a plume of white smoke curled up over the horizon,
followed by a smoke-stack like a factory chimney and the glittering thrash of water. It was one of the several large Victorian
river steamers, paddle-boats with three decks, on its regular run
from the coast to Dacca and beyond. It passed us close to with
an amount of tooting and I saw a bevy of first-class plutocratic
Pakistanis having a huge meal off blinding linen table-cloths on
the fore-deck. There was music too, a raucous wail from a small
orchestra, and a man doing tricks with a monkey. I was sorry
not to be on it. It charged upstream, an immense bellowing
thing, all set to get round the world in much less than eighty
days.

Chandpur, the tiny jute and fishing port forty miles down-
stream where we stopped, was the edge of nowhere: a rackety
corrugated town on a sandbar, yet I was told it had a population
of 250,000 and served another two million people in the
immediate area. There was a fish market, with mounds of large
grey fish piled up like cement bags, 5,000 people attempting to
board a minute ferry and an Englishwoman in a felt hat deeply
involved in a water-colour of it all.

We came upstream in the evening, cool and silent, the water
like a lake, with the country boats drifting past us, their crews
asleep or crouching around small fires in the stern—a smell of
twine and charcoal and grilled fish coming over the water which
had turned bronze and purple, with a burning orange at one end
of it. We stood on the rail looking at the sunset and the Commander talked about the tigers which get stranded in the
bamboo groves on the shifting sandbars and frighten the lives

out of the local fishermen, poking their equally startled heads out over the salt-swell and nets—and we slid into Narayanganj and drove back to Dacca.

It was the half-hour of twilight when we came into the city and the glass and the brick fragments crepitated under the wheels just as they'd done early that morning. People swarmed over the pavements and corners, taking the air as we thought, until a half-brick crashed against my door and another bounced off the roof. 'God,' said the Commander, and added a secular, naval oath. 'The language people. Trouble.' And we sped back to the hotel past armoured cars, tanks and wiry, putteed men in Home Guard helmets with Lee-Enfields and Paddy-whackers.

'My God,' two men from the Third World Conference said to me in the hotel bar that night. 'You weren't out in the streets today, were you? Two people were killed. You must be out of your mind. No one's left the hotel all day.'

'Yes. I was out. On the river. A flagship with sandwiches and 28s. 6d. worth of beer. Marvellous.'

'The river?' they said. 'A trip on the *river*?' as though I was lying or had cheated them.

'I have to get that call to Washington,' one of them said, and the other moved off for an early 'Continental supper'. The swing doors threw in another load of silk-suited refugees from the airport, the birds had a twitter in their gilded cage, the crooner couldn't give anything but love and the girls by the pool peppered their Bloody Marys and said what a bore Dacca was.

2

Wish you were here

[January 1971]

Like most of the other developing nations—an ambiguous term, that, when one thinks of the Chicago or Belfast police—India tries to pack the tourists in, playing up to the full the 'exotic East' side of its history: the Taj Mahal, the erotic temple carvings and so on. The trouble is that the country is too big, and the more popular sights are too few and far between, for the average tourist to take in, and the average tourist in this case is very often an American who is in a screaming hurry. They do the package tour of Delhi, Agra (where the Taj is) and the holy city of Benares (where the burning ghats are) and in these places the accommodation and other arrangements are excellent. But when you've seen the sights and done the bazaars in these tourist centres there is not a lot else to do. Tourism in India, if you're not very careful, is inclined to be a bit as it is in Russia: guided trips to a succession of hoary set-pieces with a desert of hotel lobbies in between. Delhi, for example, has barely any public social life at all. Everything goes on inside people's houses, or, if you are part of the large foreign community there, in their flowery back gardens over Sunday-morning gin and lime. And the tourists, when they are not out on their chain-gang safaris, are confined to barracks, marooned in their glass and concrete matchboxes—those expensive open prisons that litter the world these days and are called hotels.

All this means that to get any real idea of the country, you have to get right away from the big hotels and the packaged tours, and one of the best ways of doing this, if you have the time, is to book yourself several long round trips on Indian Railways, one of the genuine wonders of that ancient world as far as I was concerned—and much better value than the Taj Mahal. In a country with few good motor roads, railways in India are really a going concern. They make a consistent profit, are very energetically run, and there is a vast network of lines—one of the more worthwhile legacies of British rule. And since the British left, the World Bank has stepped in with vast loans to modernize and extend them. Railways and stations don't close down in India: they are building them all the time. They also build steam engines to go with them, the last country in the world to manufacture them on a production-line basis: marvellous great gleaming monsters painted in the brightest red and darkest black as if someone had rubbed too much boot polish on them.

The trains in India—with their cow-catchers and great headlights at night roaring across the plains, and the toy engines on the narrow-gauge lines winding up to the hills—can make for the most extraordinary sort of adventure, like living through an episode from the *Boy's Own Paper* in 1909. And they are exceptional value: you can travel the 800 miles from Delhi to Calcutta, first-class, air-conditioned, for about £4, with the rough and tumble of the third class a quarter of that.

Once you've paid your fare out to India, a visit there can be very cheap indeed. The B-class hotels—the sort of old colonial-commercial establishments with potted plants and wizened, tree-like retainers that you still find in most towns—are nearly always clean and good value, around £2 a day all in, which includes a mammoth English breakfast: sausages, cornflakes, kippers, marmalade, the lot. Menus for the other meals aren't half as good, and it's as well to stoke up in the morning. Unfortunately, one is inclined to get pretty tired of indifferent curries after a while (it's perfectly true, that old story about getting a better curry in the Edgware Road than in Bombay), and the so-called 'Continental' or 'English' lunch or dinner they serve is a gastronomic terror. It's nearly always clear soup, stewed chicken and blancmange, all very old, watery and tasteless—a combination which one well-known Delhi hotel is rumoured to have served up for dinner without any variation whatsoever since Queen Victoria's Diamond Jubilee.

As a foreigner, and despite the unbelievable alcoholic apartheid which prevents Indians taking a drop in public, you can get your drinks readily enough, though even the locally-made brews are wickedly expensive, while genuine Scotch whisky, that old lubricant of the Raj, costs a month's wages and is usually watered. Indian businessmen tend to carry their supplies of it about with them in large, smart briefcases, and sleep with the key under the pillow. And the drink business leads to other extraordinary stratagems. With a group of industrialists in a very posh Bombay restaurant with a three-piece string orchestra, we had lagers brought to our table in teapots: the waiter poured it out into fine bone china cups, and I thought it was cold consommé and nearly choked myself in surprise.

But to get back to the trains. When I got to India I thought the best way of seeing the country and getting out of the impossibly Grand Hotels, would be to fix myself up with a few lengthy rail safaris. So I went round to the headquarters of Indian Railways, the Rail Bhavan in New Delhi, and got a route map. 'Where do you want to go?' Mr. Dayal, one of their many very able PR officers, said to me. And later he helped me plot my course about India with all the skill of a master mariner. I certainly needed him: I had a choice of five regions, 33,000 route miles and four gauges. I could travel in any of five different classes, by steam, electric or diesel. There were 5,000 passenger trains a day, over eight million passengers in the same 24 hours going with me for company, and a permanent staff of $1\frac{1}{2}$ million to make sure I got where I was going. 'Indian Railways are really the largest anywhere,' Mr. Dayal observed, looking with a professional interest at the evening hordes cramming into buses in front of the Rail building. And I saw a poster behind his desk: 'Indian Railways: A Way of Life'. In the light of the statistics the observation didn't seem exaggerated.

The first railway in India was the Great Indian Peninsular Rail Company and it seems to have had the right sort of backing, straight from the crucible of the railway age: George Stephenson, who built the first really effective railway locomotive, 'The Rocket', was among the original directors of the company and his son Robert was appointed consulting engineer. £500,000 capital was raised in London and Messrs. Farrell and Fowler from the Midlands built the line—the twenty-one miles from Bombay to Thana which was opened in 1853, only twenty-eight years after the world's first train had made its run from Stockton to Darlington.

A history of the time relates that the local people were spellbound by the engine on its shunting trials, but not so the British residents of Bombay. In fact, there were some distinctly odd occurrences at the actual inauguration ceremony which the same book blandly doesn't explain at all. It simply quotes from the *Bombay Times* of the following day: 'The train left Bori Bunder amidst the loud applause of a vast multitude and to the salute of twenty-one guns. The Governor's band was present.' But not, apparently, the Governor himself. The report continues: 'The Governor, Lord Falkland, and the Commander-in-Chief, Lord Frederick FitzClarence, with their respective attendants, accompanied by the Bishop, the Reverend John Hardinge, left for the hills the previous evening in disregard of the memorable character of the occasion'. This first Indian engine had been named 'Falkland' too, in honour of the Governor. What had happened, one wonders, for him and his exalted retinue to have perpetrated this monumental snub? And why, on this same first run, did the other directors of the company 'take their breakfast in the Kurla tunnel'? The very uneven circumstances of this first trip to Thana seem to epitomize the British in India: a mixture of daring innovation, colossal pigheadedness and sheer eccentricity.

But, as I say, the Indians took to the rails in vast numbers from the word go, while again one reads that at the opening of the Calcutta-Hooghly line a few years later Lord Dalhousie, the Governor-General, could not undertake the journey 'on account of an indisposition'. The British seem to have behaved like children with their trains in India, scuttling off to the hills in a huff, having seen their toys commandeered by real professionals at the game. It makes me wonder if this immediate and continuing enthusiasm of Indians for trains perhaps reflects some innate psychological need of theirs—if railways, and steam engines particularly, may not appear to them as a mechanical representation of some of their philosophies: the engine's mysterious, immutable progress across the plains, like some powerful but gentle animal, seen as something to be tended and nursed, stoked and watered, to be revered, like a cow perhaps; the great spokes turning under the magic of steam, turning in a never-ending circle like the wheel of Karma; the glittering rails traversing the sub-continent, from the shrines in the hills through the places of pilgrimage, just like the holy rivers. And on the technical side, all the toy-shop, prep-school paraphernalia of the railways—the batons, bells and telegraph systems and the fiddly mysteries of single-track workings—is something which must appeal immensely to the Indian passion for bureaucracy, their obsession with form and detail. Railways are almost a religion in India, one feels, offering mystery and order to a people who crave both.

I often asked officials if there were any railway museums in India, only to be met with blank or quizzical looks. There weren't any, of course, because Indians don't look at their trains like that: they don't have to. The whole railway system is so necessary to them both economically and perhaps emotionally that there is no thought of curtailing it. Instead it expands slowly all the time, so that it is a living museum, with engines made in 1900 and the latest Indian-made electro-diesel going hand in hand on the double-line workings. Thankfully, in some ways, there are no railway buffs in India, no preservation societies: all this would be superfluous, for the whole panorama, from the great railway age of the nineteenth century to the present time, is there in front of you for the price of a ticket.

I decided I'd start by going to Simla, an overnight journey 250 miles north-west of Delhi—Simla, most imperious of hill stations and the old summer capital of the British Raj, in the foothills of the Himalayas. The 'new' New Delhi station, built in the mid-Fifties, has a ragged, battered look, already an ancient monument in ferro-concrete. And one soon sees, and feels, the reason why: the human wear and tear is fantastic. Every Indian railway station gives the impression of impending national disaster, but at Delhi and the other main-line termini things have gone a stage further: it's backs-to-the-wall close-combat stuff here, made all the more real by the fact that at least a division of the Indian Army always seems to have chosen the same train and destination as you have on any day you travel. And then there are the innumerable office wallahs, pay clerks and minor civil servants with two briefcases making their way up-country for a night, yet always accompanied by an immense retinue—a wailing Greek chorus of family, friends and colleagues —seeing them off. And besides all this there is the permanent, cactus-like human vegetation of the station—whole families and sometimes whole communities who live there, stretched out at night covered completely in sacking like corpses, and mingling with them armies of pancake and rissole men, water-carriers,

fruit vendors, scribes, fierce raggedy porters, urchins and fallen
women; these and many more have made every Indian station
their El Dorado. Then one notices the few genuine passengers,
picking their way through the debris like frightened refugees.
But what makes the whole scene bulky and prevents any movement about the station other than by means of a sort of trench
warfare is that every passenger with any pretensions at all
comes equipped for his journey with what amounts to a complete bed-sitter in miniature: an immense roll of sheets and
bedding, pots and pans and other complex domestic furniture all
rolled up to the size of fifty bolsters and strapped together with
enough rope to corral a herd of elephant.

Old guide-books to India advise you to buy this majestic piece
of equipment when you get off the steamer at Bombay—along
with your supplies of quinine and your bearers—and I'd
thought, quite wrongly, that I wouldn't need it these days. As it
was, I had to go along to the Stationmaster and hire my roll,
which turned out to be a very thin affair by comparison with
the Claridges model everyone else was sporting.

At Kalka Junction—the half-way stage next morning—we
started on the really dashing part of the journey to Simla,
changing from the ordinary broad-gauge line to the Toytown
one—the tiny two-foot-six railway that winds up the sheer sides
of the hills. Already, 2,000 feet up from the plains, there was a
distinct nip in the air. The few people about were stamping
around in mufflers and balaclavas and snow was forecast at Simla
5,000 feet beyond. A line of green pine trees stood out on the
skyline far above us and an eagle wheeled about over the sidings.
The dust and heat—the Blackpool beach of teeming India—had
quite disappeared and there was a grubby, silent air of melancholy about Kalka station, like a Midland junction in England
on a winter Sunday morning.

Our train, when it drew in, wasn't a train at all, which rather
disappointed me until I saw exactly what it was: a very imposing
Edwardian rail-car with a gracefully curved white metal sun-
shade peaking out over the huge bonnet. Inside, it was meticu-
lously finished in honey-coloured teak, grey Bournemouth blinds
with velvet tassels, and three rows of seats upholstered in red
leather. The driver sat away in the front, where the chauffeur of
a grand car would sit, and he even had a sort of metal steering-

wheel in front of him, along with an altimeter, speedometer and klaxon. The whole affair was like an eccentric Rolls-Royce that had suddenly taken to the rails—a Maharajah's railway toy, a Viceroy's mechanical litter. A red mail-bag was carefully stowed in the back seat, the doors clunked to like a cathedral closing, the klaxon brayed mournfully, the arm of a toy signal stuttered and fell in front of us, and we were off up the hills at a steady ten miles per hour.

The Simla narrow-gauge line—like the ones at Darjeeling in the north-east and at Ootacamund in the south—isn't so much a railway as an obstacle course. As a modern Indian railway guide says of it: 'During its course the line runs into a continuous succession of reverse curves of 120-foot radii in and out, the track rising in sharper curves to steeper gradients. Besides innumerable cuttings and embankments the route runs through as many as 103 tunnels in its 40-mile journey.'

The Simla line, like the others, was built with that mixture of racial conceit and great mechanical daring that characterized the British in India. Why, I wondered, take all this immense trouble to build a railway that at the time had not the slightest economic justification? And the answer was simple enough: these narrow-gauge lines were made simply to get the British Raj up off the steaming plains and into their various cool Indian Bagshots and summer parliaments. And no effort was spared in the creation of a very grand taxi service, or in making it as comfortable as possible. The predominant justification behind these lines is nicely summed up by a correspondent in a letter to the *Delhi Gazette* in November 1847. He writes about the proposed line to Simla: 'We may then see these cooler regions become the permanent seat of government, daily invigorated by a temperature adapted to refresh a European constitution, and keep the mental powers in a state of health, alike beneficial both to rulers and to ruled.' What the writer had in mind—and his successors afterwards arranged—was really a postcard from these heights to the whole Indian nation: 'Wish you were here—having a wonderful time—solely for your benefit.'

One of the many nice Victorian touches about these smaller Indian lines is that you can telegraph your lunch order forward along the line—as I'd done at Kalka Junction—so that after hours of going round the bends I was glad to crawl out of my seat and tuck into a vegetable curry at Barog, the half-way point up the mountain. And I mean crawl, for these trains really are toys as regards size.

Towards Simla, on the last lap at around 7,000 feet, the line cuts its way through a rackety Edwardian arcadia of little stations with names like Parklands and Belvedere, through embankments heavy with laurel and rhododendron, pine trees and carpets of blue wild flowers. And on the hills around were tumbling neo-gothic mansions with elaborate wooden verandas and spiky chimneys and paths running down to little private halts where the tenants of these follies ended their journeys from Delhi or Calcutta. But now one rattles straight past this dark, scented wilderness and the suburbs of Simla, past the wooden platforms with their flaking enamel advertisements that so aptly reflect the three obsessions of British India—Virol Health Extract, Stephen's Ink and Durban's Soda Water; past the decaying fortress of the first-class waiting-room and the ghosts of the Railway Children in their boaters and pinafores, playing in the gullies of the branch line, up-country in their summer place. One comes to Simla on a ghost train, by way of Curzon, Kipling and Edward VII, through the remnants of an empire at midday.

3

A summer place

[February 1971]

'There will be snow tonight, Sahib, much snow,' the porter at Clarke's Hotel in Simla said to me before I went out that afternoon to look round the town. Certainly it had become rather chilly towards the end of the 7,000-foot ascent up to Simla which I'd made that morning on the miniature, narrow-gauge railway. But snow? It didn't seem possible after the weeks of sweat I'd gone through on the plains of India below.

In the old days, when Simla was the summer headquarters of the British government in India, the Raj lived only on top of the ridge on which the little town is built—along the Mall or in one of the outlying cosy Camberleys—and now the lower slopes of this Swiss-like valley are a shanty town in wood and corrugated iron and one has to struggle up to the higher reaches to get any impression of the original idea behind the place, which was, quite simply, to build somewhere just like home, like Tunbridge Wells, say—without anything Indian, and without any Indians, who weren't allowed into the town in the old days.

One can see the remains of this architectural apartheid all along the Mall, from the severe Victorian country church and library like a public lavatory at one end—past the ornate bandstand, the Gaiety Theatre, the fire and police stations in dark granite—right down to the mecca of this old Imperial summer court: the Vice-regal Lodge a mile away in the distance. The shops on the lower Mall are almost exact copies of the English Home Counties neo-Tudor style: steeply gabled, faced in wood and plaster, with leaded glass windows. There are 'family' grocers, 'tea-shoppes' and chemists with huge coloured bottles in the window, some still with the names of their original English owners and most of them with dusty pre-war advertisements for gumboots and marmalade still prominently displayed.

This whole, utterly incongruous Cheltenham-in-the-Himalayas is still, then, very much as it was, with one appropriate but eerie difference: there isn't an English person to be seen in the place. I'd asked at the hotel that morning. 'Yes,' the manager had said, 'there is someone down the valley, a retired major. He'd be in the phone book.' I looked him up and got through, but the number went on ringing—and ringing and ringing. The phone box was next to the doorway of the hotel and I could see across the street a faded sign with 'Officers' Mess' on it. Perhaps the major had come up for his lunch and was sitting there alone, sipping a whisky, looking at the billiard cues and waiting for the telephone to ring or the door to open. But I had an appointment myself—at the Vice-regal Lodge, with Dr. Prakesh of the Indian Institute of Advanced Studies, whose headquarters the Lodge now is.

The building, at the end of a long drive flanked by innumerable gate lodges, guard-houses and garages, was extraordinary: nothing less—one of the seven wonders of the British Empire, if anyone has bothered to name, or count, the other six. Built and designed by Henry Irwin in 1888, under the Viceroyalty of the Marquis of Dufferin and Ava, it had, I was told, a room for every day of the year. But I think people say that about every palace. It was big, certainly, like a railway station—like St. Pancras, which it resembles to a certain extent. Yet it also had a certain domestic intimacy—it might have been a fine example of English neo-Gothic in the Midlands: one could easily think of an imaginative Victorian coal baron building himself such a country house in Yorkshire or Derbyshire, but not in Simla, this village, as it then was, on the Himalayan sky-line, which in 1888 was a week away from any civilization, on pack horses over a tortuous mountain road, and was often completely cut off by landslides from the rest of India.

The building exactly reflects the high-minded yet eccentric characteristics of the Victorian Empire-builders—the pig-headedness, the great structural daring and the sheer lunacy which were the hallmarks of the British in India. And these qualities reach their apotheosis in this Lodge. Yes, it's like a railway station in its necessity and usefulness as the official summer seat of the Viceroy. But it's a vague, absent-minded Lewis Carroll invention in everything else, in its absolutely *un*necessary arches and buttresses, gargoyles and towers.

The Lodge was deserted—it was between seminars at the

Institute—and after we'd had a cup of tea with the Bursar in his
ivy-shrouded annexe, Dr. Prakesh showed me round. Again, it
was the small details, not any of the grand plan, which caught
one's eye: the things which suddenly occurred without apparent
reason. I came across a minute door leading off a corner of the
ballroom, so small as to make me feel an Alice in Wonderland as
I bent down to open it. In its positioning I thought it might have
led to a pantry or a cloakroom. Instead I found a small clogged
space littered with half-opened parcels of pre-war *Country Life*,
a boxful of Union Jacks on tiny sticks, and scattered copies of
The Monkey's Paw in French's amateur acting edition. In the
middle of all this rubbish was a beautifully ornate, again minute,
winding staircase in richly carved teak. I had started to go up it
before Dr. Prakesh shouted that the top was blocked off and I
wouldn't get anywhere. What was it? I asked him. 'An escape
for the Viceroy,' he said. 'Or the Vicereine. The stairway led up
to her bedroom above.' It had been a way of making an unregal
getaway at the ball, or of avoiding someone you didn't want to
meet. You danced around to that corner of the room and then
just disappeared. Like magic. And could it have had other, less
diplomatic uses too, I wondered? An inconspicuous entrance to
her Ladyship's chambers for some dashing Flashman? Simla was
a notorious place for losing your husband, or your wife: a giddy
zone of infidelity after a hard spell of marital duty on the plains.

The ballroom had been turned into the Institute's library, but
some of the other rooms had been preserved exactly as they were:
little English domestic sanctuaries in the midst of offices and
classrooms for advanced studies, endless volumes of commentary
on Hindu texts and miles of Indian Parliamentary papers. One
such room was the Vicereine's bedroom, which we saw later.
Everything in it had been left untouched, Dr. Prakesh said:
the silver-backed hand mirrors and powder bowls on the dress-
ing-table, coloured engravings of the Quorn Hunt and two
chamber-pots emblazoned decoratively with some Viceroy's
arms. 'Nothing has been touched,' Dr. Prakesh exclaimed
proudly, 'except the mirror. We took away the mirror.' 'What
mirror?' I asked. 'There,' and he pointed to a huge, empty
wooden frame which lay along the top of the four-poster bed.

Next there was the tiny dressing-room on the first floor by
the grand staircase where Lord Mountbatten, Nehru and

Mahomed Jinnah had between them divided up India in the explosive summer of 1947. This too had been left exactly as it was: a lot of floppy, chintzy armchairs, a small table in the middle and three sound-proofed green baize doors, two of them specially built for reasons of protocol, since all the parties had naturally insisted on having their own separate entrances into this minute dressing-room.

I wondered what Nehru and Jinnah had made of it all during those blazing terrible months when they stayed here arguing the toss. The aristocratic, country-house mood of the place might have been expected to cool their tempers, induce reflection and calm. And yet I can just as well see how Simla and this Lodge might have induced anger and mistrust: the Hindus have their temples, replicas of their faith, in which sensuality and belief are inextricably mixed. And so too the English have their temples, their country houses, even in the Himalayas, in which their real absorptions and character are mirrored—their insular arrogant *je m'en foutisme*. Such qualities, so epitomized in the Lodge, could well have infuriated Nehru and Jinnah, especially Nehru, that tortured half-Englishman, while the nip in the air of pine and laurel, like an expensive deodorant, may not have pleased the lethargic Moslem temperament of Jinnah's entourage, if not Jinnah himself. Mountbatten, one must suppose, was reasonably at ease in these English airs—or did he too loathe the chintzy pomp, the brigades of under-butlers and turbaned bearers, the whole incongruity of this Bagshot on the roof of the world? Strangely enough, his own house, Classiebawn Castle in the west of Ireland, is not unlike the Lodge: another Victorian Gothic fairy-tale affair, standing out like a Rackham silhouette on an eminence over the Atlantic.

Downstairs, on the three basement levels of the Lodge, were the laundries, kitchens and storerooms, full of broken furniture and unbelievable regal bric-à-brac: more chamber-pots—with the Royal arms on them this time—dog carts, wardrobes of English and Indian riding livery, smashed Budge Patty tennis rackets, tarnished plated-silver cocktail shakers, libraries of Mazo de la Roche, and all the other necessities of those long-ago summers.

On the final floor were the dungeons: long rows of savage iron cages, dark, dripping, windowless—the black holes of Simla. In the corner of one of the cages there was a gigantic pile of very old boot-polish tins, stamped with the emblem and legend of the Army and Navy Stores. I was rather surprised by all this. Wasn't there a very substantial jail in the town? I asked Dr. Prakesh. 'Oh yes,' he said. 'But this one was for the Indians who were caught on the estate. Poachers and so on.' Dozens of poachers, I thought, cleaning dozens of pairs of boots.

But the really remarkable thing about the Viceregal Lodge is how a present-day generation of Indians have preserved the place almost intact, and how ready, proud even, many were to talk about it all. There was, of course, a suitable measure of diatribe in their responses: phrases like 'Imperial yoke' and 'the boot of the oppressor' occurred here and there. But essentially their opinions about the British in India were full of an imperfectly expressed nostalgia, a sense of conflicting allegiances. One could describe such people, I suppose—in the gadfly tones of that marvellous Indian writer Nirad Chaudhuri—as Anglicized Hindus of the old brigade. The only difficulty is, though, that these Indians were *not* elderly. They were in their thirties and sometimes younger—the *sons* of the Harrow Indians.

I wonder if the British represent for these people a discipline and sense of purpose which India has not yet managed to provide them with? And so they remember the British with a perverse affection, a subconscious desire to emulate them, and, if one agrees with Chaudhuri's theories on the Hindu migration to India, with a racial nostalgia as well. 'We too were Europeans. We too colonised India, before you came, and hounded the Dravidians into the hills. We were—we are—like you.' Such a theory goes a long way to explaining the extraordinary Indian tendency to parody everything English: in accent, word usage, clothes, reading-matter, and in the structure of their academic, cultural and social life. What's coming to the surface here, in this exaggerated addiction to 'good form', polo, tweeds and the English Lake Poets, is a latent belief whose creed is: 'Not only are we like you—we are more like you than you are yourselves.'

The Hindus were from the beginning *déraciné* in India, as conquerors and colonizers, so that when we speak of an Anglicized Hindu we may be speaking simply of those Hindus who are feeding a race memory of their previous grandeur in the sub-continent. This seems to me partly to explain their schizophrenic affection for the British. The two races are sisters under the skin: plunderers and lords of all creation together in the same continent, separated in their arrogance only by time. So they preserve the Royal Arms, the emblazoned VR over the porch at Viceregal Lodge, the Officers' Mess off the Mall downtown in Simla, and much else of British India, as a reminder of their own lost empires, of the powerful days when as Curzons and Kiplings and Edward the Sevenths they lorded it over a now forgotten Hindu dominion.

Dr. Prakesh took me up to the roof of the Lodge and showed me the washed-away lines of a hard tennis court that had been built on top of the north wing, looking down on a tangled ornamental garden with broken statuary and overgrown laurel and rhododendron walks stretching away into the hills. It was coming to evening and huge shadows a mile long crawled up the pine forest in the valley below the Lodge, and after the shadows a white mist rose, like a lake of milk, dissolving the blue-black colours of the huge landscape. The church clock in Simla rang out six times, the small Home Counties music lost at once in the background of crowded hills.

We crawled down through the cisterns and the rafters, I said goodbye and made my way back up the Mall. There was no one around. An Indian—a mysterious fellow in a cloth coat with a Gladstone bag—whirled down the empty hill road in a trishaw, two ragged men in front and another acting as brake at the back; the spokes whirring round, hammering on the cobbles, like a hansom cab. Fires had been lit all over the lower slopes of the town; there was a sudden crisp, sweet smell like turpentine and baked apples in the air, and I remembered the old hall porter's dour warning earlier in the day: 'There will be snow tonight, much snow.'

And sure enough, later that night it came, light and flaky, drifting in from the Himalayas, across the Mall, over the shanty town and down the hill. It piled over the gables of the Tudor shops and around the entrance to the theatre with its old production photographs of *Blithe Spirit* and *Quiet Weekend*; it flaked over the marmalade advertisements in the shop windows and edged its way into the lattice-work of the bandstand and covered all one side of the steeple. And when I came back from a last stroll, the three coaching-lamps over the hotel porch winked at me through the white flutter like a Christmas card.

4

The face at the window

I was meeting an Indian friend on my first evening in Delhi—in one of those concrete matchbox Grand Hotels that are everywhere today. The mood in the lobby was antiseptic, anonymous, vaguely worrying; it was like being in the charge room of heaven: nothing individual or eccentric, nothing human, and hardly anything Indian.

My friend was late so I thought I'd wait for him in the bar. Apart from a pretty tipsy American at one end I was the only customer and fairly soon I was talking to Mr. Gupta, the barman. He was human enough. He wasn't happy with his work, he said. He was emigrating to Canada this winter. He'd got a job there, with a firm that made business machines. Why? I asked. He was an engineering graduate and couldn't get any sort of decent job in India—that was why. My friend arrived and I asked him what he was having.

'I'm sorry, sir, we can't serve Indians' Mr. Gupta interjected in a soft voice. 'It's not a dry day, I know, but we're not allowed to serve Indians on *any* day here in Delhi.' The American at the other end of the bar called for another large martini. I couldn't finish my beer in rage and astonishment.

'I should have warned you,' my friend said afterwards, 'not to meet in bars. It's very embarrassing for us. And I can't take you to my club either. There's a new law about not serving drinks to guests—Indian or otherwise.'

'But haven't you made a fuss about it?' I asked. 'I mean, the idea of serving me, that American, of serving anyone else but you, an *Indian*—it's incredible. How do you put up with it?'

'There's nothing to be done,' he said. 'It's the way things are here. It's better to do nothing—just steer a course of your own.'

The Grand Hotel had turned out to be not so anonymous after all. It had been pretty instructive: no work for qualified engineers, no drink for qualified Indians, a drunk American and a

64

mystified visitor. What was one to make of a country that so discriminated against its own nationals in this way?—and worse, the apparent apathy about it all, or protest in the shape of a boat to Canada. Still, I thought, I'd find things different—a more positive approach—when I got around the place a bit more. I didn't. Though I did find, in small pockets at least, more vociferous complaints about the way things were run.

More vociferous complaints?—520 million silent complaints perhaps. I've not seen Louis Malle's documentary films about India: perhaps if I had I might have a clearer idea of why I found the country so mysteriously depressing—mysterious because it's not the people starving or dying in the gutter who alone create this feeling, appalling though their condition is; it's something else altogether.

Perhaps I'll have to start by saying, bluntly, that many Indians—and by no means only the impoverished ones—seem to me to have completely lost their identity as human beings. They are moving, robot like, through a world they never made and which, in turn, was never intended for them—no more than animals were meant for zoos; that is to say that one has the impression of a complete rupture in the natural order of things, a feeling of an utterly absurd world in India—a continent rather than a café of existentialism: an incontrovertible fact, rather than any argument, of that philosophy.

And one senses this in every view: in the incredibly weary faces everywhere, an almost palpable fatalism—apathy, detachment, despair: the look in their eyes—so eloquently expressive of the fact that life has become an utter and complete treadmill, and that they are perfectly aware it shouldn't have been like this. It was apathy mixed with a glimmer of long lost ambition, a face at the window looking in on everything it had lost or never had. Unlike people in rather the same condition who I've come across in other parts of the developing world—in South-East Asia and Africa—many Indians seemed acutely aware of their hell, steeped in it. There was an active quality in their despair; the kind of sour, moody restlessness found among long-term prisoners in the spring. They were disenchanted, horror stricken, with their whole physical world—and it was a life sentence.

Previously there may have been the consolations of their faith but among the huge urban population at least this has been largely destroyed by extreme materialist ambitions, a thirst for western ways and means—the faith of the spin dryer and the automatic corkscrew—a search for the sort of Western status which only a minute proportion of people in India will ever enjoy, leaving the rest to crave for them, faces pressed against the window, in an ever increasing momentum of envy and despair.

This is what 'development'—our sort of development—has come to mean in a place like India; a 'rising tide of expectations' in Adlai Stevenson's words, and I think it's implicit in them that he didn't expect them to be met. That was ten years ago—and they've not been: the expectations have simply grown more violently clamorous.

Stevenson, I think, like far too few others in the West, doubted the efficacy of our technological skills and moral precepts in the third world. And I'm sure he was right, though I can't say I have any burning alternative to offer. All I would say is that, in the present circumstances, the more Westernized Indians become, the more 'aid' they receive, then the more de-natured, envious and unhappy they are likely to be. And one can apply this formula all over the developing world, or not, as one chooses. At any rate one should ask: is this what we mean by development?—the creation of explosive, unrequited expectations. It's one of the many *a priori* questions which the developers, so busy developing, don't seem to have asked themselves.

What I'd like to do here is to try and find some reasons for this deep Indian depression, and to trace how Western influence in India, to my mind, has consistently furthered rather than alleviated it; to try and show how our views of 'development' in India and elsewhere have been largely misguided, usually misapplied and will almost certainly result in the creation of the very circumstances the development was intended to avoid.

The Hindus, I would argue, are a homeless people in India, which has given them a high disatisfaction and envy quotient from the beginning. They are an Aryan race, latterly from Iran, who colonized northern India somewhere around 1000 B.C., driving the native Dravidians into the hills. Yet as colonizers, unlike the British, they never seem to have become reconciled to the country or to have organized themselves comfortably in it. They seem to have been defeated by their surroundings there. In the arid plains there was a never satisfied longing in them for the greener pastures west of the Euphrates which they'd left. This historical schizophrenia between the 'now' and 'then' of their lives must lie close to the reason for the Hindu tendency to swing violently between extremes today; between sensuality and aceticism, cowardice and bravery, the shabby and the magnificent. One only has to take one issue—that of the Indian Prince's Privy Purses—to see this latter pendulum in action. Of course it would have been entirely right to curtail a feudal arrangement which favoured the already very rich against the completely impoverished. No one, not even the Princes I think, would have questioned that—had that been the issue. But it wasn't.

The issue at stake was that the Indian government itself in 1947, in return for the Prince's states and the various fiscal privileges which went with them, agreed to pay them an annual pension by way of compensation, worth very much less than the financial and other interests which the Princes had surrendered in the cause of a united India. Yet the wrangle has been presented as an example of the Indian government's dedication to proper democratic processes—to western processes, as they are. In fact it is merely evidence of their extraordinary bad faith, fully in tune with the same sort of political expediency practised in the mother of parliaments—on which, of course Indians have based their own.

And with it they have taken on all the other glittering clichés of Western progress: nuclear plants, high dams, capital intensive agriculture—the so-called 'green revolution': a revolution indeed which has made millionaires out of the already rich farmers and pushed the others even further into the dust. Of course large holdings are more economic to develop and give much higher yields per acre. The point is though, forgotten in a windfall of hybrid seeds, that 95 per cent of the population in India does things in a *small* way, as farmers or artisans, so for them this splendid development has gone on not only quite above their heads—it has further depressed their already precarious livelihood. Is this 'development'? Surely it is the reality behind the phrase 'being dragged screaming into the twentieth century'— our century, the Western century.

Above all the Indians have learnt from us the skills of

democratic appeasement, and with it, in the Indian situation, all the violence which must ensue from such a policy.

The Princes, for example, had the power and the opportunity to split the continent down the middle twenty-three years ago. The electorate have that same leverage today: hence the Princely sacrifice. But tomorrow the prohibition lobby will have to be placated—the day after the Brewers and the Toddy Tappers Association. One has to run from logic here, far from any conception of genuine public good—*everyone* has to be pleased so that in the end no one really is.

One may say that this is inevitable and just, that it's the democratic treadmill—a little at a time, very slowly. And that would be fair comment, except for one thing: there is nothing like enough time left in India to work things out that way. Proper democracy, with its inherent checks and balances, is based on time. What use is such a system if in the end it presides over skeletons? Would we then think it such an admirable gift?

The point about what the British 'gave' to India—whether it was law, or good government or railways—was that it was backed up with machine-gun platoons and engineers from Doncaster and Sheffield—by the Werner Von Brauns from the Cape Kennedys of the day: it was never so much a gift as a threat. And the present technological invasion in India, albeit devoutly encouraged by their present rulers, seems to me the same. There have been improvements certainly, monumental improvements—and probably in the end about as appropriate and useful. But there has been *no* improvement in the face at the window—which appears as emaciated and despairing as ever. The Indian depression, instead of lifting, lowers.

I think of British New Delhi as an excellent example of one of the stations on the Indian cross—their calvary on the way to 'enlightenment'.

Designed by Lutyens, started in 1911 and never completed, what a marvellous conceit it none the less is. How spacious, well ordered and clean—how few people about. With its creeper-shrouded villas on wide tree-lined avenues radiating out in huge spokes from India Gate it's more reminiscent of Hausmann's Paris than anything else, a genuine Elysium field. The architecture is so incredibly confident and overbearing that it works. The scale of everything is gargantuan. One sees a lot of high-minded Edwardian children playing a game called 'Empire' on a board marked 'India'—and going mad with rulers and great slabs of granite and red sandstone. The result is invigorating, splendid, but it's not India. It bears no relevance to that continent now at all. Yet at the time how it was venerated: it was the shrine of the 'better life', a cornucopia of good intentions, the epicentre of progress. Of course the Indians didn't care for the outward and visible form of this faith and the missionaries were eventually dispatched. But their message was retained as Gospel by the new Raj: a little at a time, very slowly, in terms of genuine development; and a lot, very quickly, in terms of prestige investment—nuclear power stations and so on.

Finally for India there is the new western miracle: international and unilateral aid, whose outposts are not Viceregal lodges but organizations abbreviated into almost every letter in the alphabet. Are these, and their millions, bringing a smile to the face at the window? In three months' travelling about India for one such organization I can't say I saw it. A grimace or two, yes, and a laugh from the profiteers.

Aid, unfortunately, can only be as effective as is the government which must implement it. Secondly, it will reflect *their* priorities, not the donors. An ineffective government with the wrong priorities will turn aid into a minus factor at once. To take one aspect of aid to India where, in this way, it has aggravated the very problems it might have been expected to alleviate: population and the urban disaster. For the past twenty years Delhi's priorities as regards Gupta Sen have been to give him a crash course in heavy industry and to defend him against possible, but unlikely, attack from Karachi or Peking. Hence the aid has largely gone to build industrial plant which has released an equal amount of money for sabre rattling—to defending the northern frontiers and cossetting the armed forces with the most sophisticated and expensive weaponry available. In 1968, in fact, the income and expenditure in these two fields balanced each other out almost exactly: India received nearly £500 million overall in aid and spent the same amount on defence. Ironic surely?—yet even so the priorities may strike you as fair enough. But if you look behind them, there is the fatal equation: factories are not built in fields; they are tacked on to already bursting cities or form the nucleus for new ones: the more you

industrialize, the more urbanization you create, the more people
there are, the more slums you have—the more poverty, ignorance and despair. You have helped, not hindered, that chain
reaction which ends in a population explosion, bringing with it
violence and unrest, the ghettos of 'rising expectations'. You
have exacerbated beyond measure the human horror of urban
India in exchange for a steel mill or two.

Meanwhile you have dedicated an equal amount of money
and energy to defending this state of affairs. That has been the
'development' and it has been substantially at the hands of our
'aid'.

And in agriculture one can easily find the same sort of perver-
sion of aid. I remember coming across an expert from one of the
international agencies in the middle of India where a costly and
extensive irrigation scheme had been introduced years previously.
His speciality was communications, not agronomy or livestock
control as one might have expected. What was he communicat-
ing, I asked him? 'I'm trying to help get it across to the local
people that the canal water is for *them*, not just the landlords,
that they can take feeder channels from it for their own patch of
ground. They've never believed that before.' The aid, in this
case, had been properly directed but no one had followed it up
with explanations to the smallholders on how to make proper
use of it—thus further inflaming the hatred and unrest of the
agrarian poor in the area.

As one Indian economist recently put it: 'Indian planners
have unwittingly created, in a decade and a half of hard work,
not the promised socialist millennium, but near ideal laboratory
conditions for the spread of communism.'

Clearly that economist wasn't hoping for Marx; clearly he is
as disenchanted with Moscow and Washington as he is with the
'new socialism' of his own planners. He was intent, I think, on
simply recognizing and correctly defining present conditions,
on seriously considering the fate of those despairing faces. There
are so few of him in India and so many of the others.

5

Gumboots east of Suez

[September 1970]

We're supposed to be getting out of Singapore next year and, as usual, we're much more upset about it all than the locals are—the locals who, unusually in this case, are making odd, sad, suitable noises about our departure but are surely rubbing their hands quietly at the prospect of all that marine and RAF equipment about to fall into their laps.

A look at the map tells you the crucial thing about Singapore, as it told Stamford Raffles in the old gunboat days of Empire a 150 years ago: Singapore is right bang in the middle of South-East Asia, is the axis of a dozen countries and trade routes, and it will obviously sink or swim in that geographic and political context in the years to come. Despite Sir Alec's strong rearguard action, the Dreadnoughts have in fact gone, along with the *Boy's Own Paper* and the Nine O'Clock News—and I think the locals have known this for a long time, at least since the battleships 'Prince of Wales' and 'Repulse' were sunk off Malaya in 1941 and the Japs came roaring down the peninsula and across onto the island where all the guns were pointing the wrong way.

Raffles, with great tenacity and vision in the teeth of the usual apathy from Whitehall, founded the colony in 1819 and the British presence on the island since then has, of course, been the reason behind its present prosperity. But the Imperial party is over, despite the stragglers being encouraged now to gobble at the remnants of the feast; it's long been time for us to go, and when I went to Singapore I'd really come to see how we were managing to get our hats and coats together.

The Cockpit Hotel, a mansion in the grandest Palladian-Colonial style, is on a rise above the city and the taxi sloshed and skidded up the hill. It had been raining on the island for days, I was told, and it went on in the same way for most of my time there: real Turkish bath rain, the water steaming as it fell—as it did for hours on end without the slightest variation in the

71

'pour', straight down in unending grey lines, as though organized from above by a slide rule.

I sat in the bar of the Cockpit Hotel on my first evening and watched two English men writing on bits of paper with piles of Strait's Dollars beside them and looking out at the downpour on the terrace every so often. They were betting, to the nearest minute, on when the rain would stop—as apparently it did, like a tap being turned off. But it hadn't done so an hour later and by that time, in some desperation, I was sliding down the hill again and into the town.

Rain indeed. The title of one of Somerset Maugham's plays—though it wasn't set here, I don't know why. I started to think of that ace chronicler of the region, wondering where all his 'fables of the exotic East' had got to, as I made my way un-hopefully to the Raffles Hotel through a hurricane, the wind whipping the tops of the marvellous Emperor palms in the hotel forecourt about like ostrich feathers under Niagara.

The Hotel fronted onto the 'Victory Club'—NAAFI Far East G.H.Q. or something, and the very worst piece of public lavatory architecture I've ever seen. Grey and featureless and foreboding and sodden with a few bedraggled sailors sheltering with girls on the pavement and being pestered by trishaw drivers in old army macs. It might have been a Monday night in Solihull.

The Raffles was huge and empty and as romantic as an empty bingo hall. The original Spanish-courtyard design of the hotel seems to have been expanded in a most appalling way—a great wavy-roofed, ferro-concrete annexe tacked onto the front, as big as a football pitch with two deserted tent-like bars at either end, like the ones you get at small point-to-points. Two sailors were drinking cups of tea in the middle of it—with piles of money and bits of paper beside them. They were playing one of the many indoor games for foreigners in Singapore. The rain tumbled on the roof and they looked up and listened to it intently every now and then, like punters in the Ark.

But there was another, older bar behind in the original hotel, with Elizabethan armorials round the walls, leather chairs, deep mahogany panelling and brilliant linen napkins every-where—an old Empire sanctuary where the fruit for the Pimms came in silver buckets and the counter reeked deliciously—soaked in generations of strong gin and lemon peel. And here I met Signor Marchesi, the most agreeable manager of the hotel.

'The Rain, yes,' he said. 'Yes.' And he left it at that with a perfect Roman gesture of acceptance.

Later we talked about Maugham. Signor Marchesi had been under-manager at the time of Maugham's last visit around his Shangri-la's of South-East Asia in the mid-'Fifties.

'He was so polite,' Signor Marchesi remembered. 'And delicate. Like porcelain. You thought he'd break at any moment. But he thought and talked like a young man. That's what surprised me. Perhaps being back here gave him something of his youth. Perhaps. Not that there's much left of his city here now. Brrrr ... Brrrr ... Brrrr ...' He mimed a power drill.

'"Raffles Hotel—Stands for all the fables of the exotic East",' I read out from the menu card on the counter.

'Yes,' Signor Marchesi said. 'I wrote to him about that—it's from one of his books. A charming reply.'

'I suppose he wasn't thinking of the rain thing, though,' I said. 'In the fine weather I expect he meant. That would be more the fable time ...'

Somehow I'd not been prepared for so much rain in Singapore. I thought all the hurricane stuff would be up-country, with rubber planters being driven wild with passion by 'Lilac Time' on a gramophone, and a girl from Sunningdale, and walking out into the storm with sou'westers and heavy service pistols.

'I suppose—I've come at the wrong time,' I said, as though I'd come 10,000 miles for a party and got the wrong day. 'There's always Bugis Street,' another man said who'd joined us. 'I don't think you need worry much about the weather there.' Signor Marchesi lent me a mackintosh and I put my money in my shoe.

Bugis street isn't mentioned in any of the excellent guides to Singapore: it's a shabby, harshly lit lane, just along from the Raffles, with wooden balconied shanties and pavement cafés right down along its length. A rough and tumble sort of place with garish pop music, sailors and a lot of carousing from litre beer bottles: just the spot for a first paragraph in a Jack London story.

In fact the traditional vices are mild to a degree in Bugis street and the first thing I found myself doing when I got a table was playing noughts and crosses for 20 cent pieces with a cluster of delightful Chinese children with blackberry eyes and pencil fringes who make a living out of this—and often, like Russian chess masters, playing two or three games simultaneously with a group of customers. They never lost.

No, Bugis street is not the centre for opium or cannabis, or exchanging Chinese yen, or getting contraband or drunk. Although you *can* do all these things here, Bugis street is really for something else altogether: it's where you sit and watch some of the most astonishingly attractive girls anywhere parading up and down—girls of bewildering beauty: some with pale Italianate faces with dark curves of hair circling their cheeks, and others blonde and sunburnt—and high-cheeked Malayan and Chinese girls with dazzling cheongsams cut half-way up their thigh. And they walked up and down that night through the rain as though it was a sprinkler on the set for a Gene Kelly film, flowery and un-pushy and fragile with tulip-leaved umbrellas and scarlet vinyl macs, and one girl had a cocker spaniel on a lead.

The sailors looked at them, quietly astonished—forgetting their beers and the noughts and crosses and the Indians selling 'Dunhill' pipes made in Hong Kong—looking at them without facetiousness or laughter, just with unbelief. And I knew why. Bugis street is Drag Row in South East Asia and every single one of the girls was a man.

That was a bit more like the exotic East, I thought, as I paddled back to the Cockpit Hotel. The two English men were still at the bar and things were now alcoholically as well as climatically sodden. There'd not been the slightest let up in the downpour and it looked as if they intended to sit out the rainy season over lengthening odds. The next morning I was going off to take a look at the RAF base at Changi on the eastern tip of the island, to see how the British were getting on with getting out, or thinking of getting out, and by midday I was under arrest for my pains.

I'd arranged to meet the base publicity officer at the guardhouse by the main gate and was surprised enough on stepping up to the reception desk to see three Malays lined up facing the wall, hands high, being frisked by two gentlemen with Stenguns. There was a notice behind the Sergeant's desk cautioning base personnel 'not to talk to strangers'—'the walls have ears' and so on.

I identified myself at the double, shot my cuffs, straightened my tie and lit a cigarette. I reflected on the dubious advantage of being six feet four, palefaced and smartly turned out in my linen tropicals. I clearly wasn't a 'stranger' in these parts. But another gun-toting, red-band boy scout bore down on me. 'No smoking, sir,' and my man would be down in a minute and there was a security check on.

The three Malays were marched off to the cells, Mr. Brice the deputy P.R. Officer arrived and in a moment we were buzzing round Changi camp, a huge complex of buildings and roads laid out like a tropical golf course on various hills called after various aeronautic worthies and with asphalt paths grandly named Hendon road, Cranwell road and Biggin Hill road.

We saw the famous Changi murals done by Bombardier Stanley Warren in St. Luke's Chapel during the war when Changi was a Japanese prison camp—and we saw a copy of a poem called 'The Corporal and his Pal' in memory of two Australian soldiers who had escaped the camp and were afterwards summarily executed by the Japanese:

'They murdered him in hatred
Prolonged his tortured end.
In spite of all his pleadings
They turned and shot his friend.
They said he was example
of what they had in store
For others who attempt escape
Whilst prisoners of war.
Examples, yes—of how to die,
And how to meet one's fate.
Example, true—of selfless love
A man has for his mate.'

Afterwards there was a mid-morning beer at the Angling Club looking over the Johore straits where there was much despondency over their monthly allowance of duty-free beer, which had recently been cut by something like a thousand gallons. What the allowance could have been in the first place I didn't ask. The Club committee had an interesting system of preserving their quota by only allowing the pints tax-free before twelve o'clock, when most of the men came off duty I imagined, and the few of us there drank steadily for exactly 43 minutes, eyes rooted to the clock.

Brice and I were just making our way quietly along Hendon road for an inspection of the hospital before lunch when a West Indian corporal jumped over Temple Hill at us with a Sten-gun and told us to get out of the car. We did, rather falling over ourselves, and I heard his gun click like a knuckle breaking. There was no one about and it looked like rain again.

'God,' I thought, and wondered about the air freight for bodies back to England and did one really have to go in a lead-lined coffin.

Identity papers. My friend Brice was in civvies and my linen tropicals were well crumpled now and I had the air of an unsteady remittance man.

'Um, er, well, er . . .'

I never heard so many ums and ers from a P.R. man.

'This is Mr. Hone,' Brice said eventually. 'Visiting journalist, a little bit of colour material on how we're all doing here . . .'

'Your papers . . .'

We didn't seem to have any.

'Well you see it's like this,' Brice said, 'the car wouldn't start this morning an—'

'Yes!' I piped in. 'And what excellent security you've got here—absolutely A1, on the ball. And you're doing a splendid job yourself I shall certainly want to tell the folks back home about that. What's your name and number?—and very nice of you too. We were just on our way to lunch . . .'

The corporal marched us down Hendon road and into Cranwell road at gunpoint.

'What sort of lunch *do* you get here by the way—quite decent?' I chatted to Brice on the way down the hill. 'Steak and all that? A little local wine?—hardly I suppose. Though they make an excellent gin from bananas in Uganda . . .'

'I don't know what sort of lunch we'll be having,' Brice replied quietly and sharply.

An Australian officer and half a dozen Military Police were busily playing games with coloured pins and going through a lot of gobbledegook on field telephones when we got to the guard house.

'Found them on Hendon road, Sah. Making for the Hospital. No papers.'

The men dropped their coloured pins and went quiet, like unlucky anglers seeing the float duck for the first time, and waiting a second before the strike: gleaming red outdoor faces, blancoed belts, highland knees—the sort of Antipodean men who'd fell an oak or shear a sheep in sixty seconds dead.

'I'm Brice, Deputy P.R.—and this is Hone. We were—looking round the camp.'

It didn't sound at all good. It was back at school with surnames only and a tricky housemaster.

'We were going for a spot of lunch actually. I hear you've got some marvellous fish around here . . .'

'Drop them, drop them,' I thought the Australian officer said. Some free-fall, non-parachute affair I thought—to get the truth out of us—before I realized he'd said 'Drop in, drop in' in thick Darwinese, or he may have come from Sydney Hill.

'Sorry to bother you. We have to stop everybody. Just a bad day. Have to hold you till we get confirmation from Main Gate.' Well, the main gate must have been under siege by irate Malays for we stayed there almost an hour.

'Do you like it here?' I asked the officer at one point.

'Marvellous bloody place. Be sorry to leave.'

'Well I won't,' I added and I straightened my tie again.

Eventually they let us out, but not before I heard some sort of alarm go off over towards the Married Families Quarters and Alsatians whimpering excitedly.

Lunch was over when we got to the Officer's Club.

'Sorry, sir. I can give you a plate of chips with—'

'That's all right,' Brice interrupted, 'we'll have a whisky.'

'Sorry, sir. Bar's closed . . .'

Suddenly the weather cleared up, a siren whined an all clear and the Married Families streamed out onto the beach below the Club in zebra-patterned trunks and bikinis. They blew up their lilos and dabbled in the Riviera shallows, got the lotion out and the transistors on. The sun really burst out, for the first time since I'd arrived in Singapore—baking out of the bluest sort of sky on all the happy families. A motor boat started up with a roar from somewhere beyond the Angling Club and I thought of asking Brice if they had water skiing here as well. But the question might have sounded sarcastic and I didn't want to appear shortsighted about the morning's difficulties. There was, after all, months—perhaps years—before sunset on this little Empire. Instead, I wondered if they'd let the three Malays out of the guardhouse yet—or were they another piece of real estate not due for repatriation until we'd made our minds up.

PART THREE

Africa

1

The Animals

[September 1968]

Beyond those trees—Acacia trees, Fever trees, what are they? I've not been here long enough to know—anyway, somewhere out there, between the line of trees and the great blue and white shoulder of Mount Kilimanjaro which rises sheer from the plain like an optical illusion fifteen miles away—are the animals.

We've not seen any yet, just a few gazelle in the far distance —not the animals we've come to see: lion, rhino, elephant.

It's early morning. We've just left camp, with its steaming pots of coffee, the first cigarettes like mist in the air, and people groping round in the half light with mufflers, for it was icy cold then. Now, a few hours later, it's the best part of the day in Africa: just comfortably hot. A soft wind flaps my hair in my face, the wheels of the lorry swish through the tall grass, sometimes thumping over an old elephant track which has hardened since the rains, sometimes raising a covey of sand grouse who clatter away across the grass like stones flipping over a lake.

No one says anything.

By midday the whole landscape will have become a searing blaze of dust and light; the greys and golds of dawn, the blues, the yellows of the plain, will all have disappeared along with the animals and there'll be plenty of time to chat then.

Now, standing up at the back of the lorry, everyone looks around them—across these miles of empty rangeland with its islands of scrub and trees and small hills, and it's exactly like being on the bridge of a ship moving across a calm sea.

At first I can't see anything to our right about two hundred yards away. The others, the wildlife students who've come with us on this safari, don't take much notice. What is it? A rhino— a lion perhaps—difficult to see against the dun-coloured scrub. How on earth can they see it, whatever it is—so easily—and I can't? Extraordinary. There's nothing there. Then as we get nearer, the scrub, the trees, start to move: a large herd of giraffe, perfectly camouflaged until then, start to amble off with great gangling strides, but perfectly balanced, appropriate, like a waltz in slow motion.

Of course, what surprised me was their moving like this at all —although I'd seen them often in zoos—until I realized that in zoos giraffes don't run like this; they can't, there isn't enough room.

Later, half a mile away from the lorry, I suddenly see hundreds of black shapes rising and falling above the grass, like porpoises careering over a yellow sea—and then a growling thunder which lasted until long after the shapes had disappeared.

'Buffalo,' someone remarks casually.

A first morning in the African bush, a first look at the animals in their real landscape—even they were doing nothing remarkable—was one of the most remarkable things I'd ever experienced. And of course this has been true—will be true—for many others. Never before has there been so much interest in African wildlife—in killing it, preserving it, photographing it and reading about it. Why? For obvious reasons—these are beautiful creatures we no longer have in our own continents— and some not so obvious. Dr. Bernard Grziemk in his book *Serengeti shall not die* touches on one of them when he says, talking about the gradual disappearance of wildlife everywhere: 'People feel that something belonging to their lives has been taken from them, and their souls bear the scars.'

Well, what exactly has been taken from us? And what are the obviously compelling attractions of these animals, this primeval landscape of East Africa where they are still to be found? Is it really life as it was before the fall—or is this just an idea of Africa we get from the animal films and the picture books? These were some of the questions that interested me when I spoke to people who had spent most of their lives in the bush dealing with animals: game wardens, wildlife instructors, professional hunters—people who've felt deeply about the place they live in, the life they share with the animals. But for me, coming to East Africa for the first time, it was quite different. I'd no intention of writing about the wildlife there—anything else but. The animals had been over-exploited already, I thought —over-sentimentalized, over-done altogether. And it was a good time to look at some other aspect of the area.

As it turned out I failed. It was impossible to avoid dealing with the animals—indeed running into them on journeys to look at other things in Kenya. Late at night, coming back from a model farm in Masailand, a herd of elephant reared up in front of the car so that we braked only inches from their enormous, wrinkled backsides and sat there with hearts stopped while they trumpeted a little round the car and swung their trunks about and flapped their ears before lurching off noiselessly into the bush; a leopard caught in the headlights one night, its eyes still and luminous for a moment, malevolent and strange, before it bounded away at incredible speed up the road; a large snake we crunched over a week later on the way to Uganda . . .

There is no question that the wildlife in East Africa *must* involve the visitor, sooner or later, even if he's only come there to sell aspirin. In economic terms alone the animals have become vitally important. After coffee, tourism in Kenya is the next largest source of foreign revenue—and it's expected to outdo the coffee in a few years' time. But still, I wondered if I should get involved.

'Aren't you going to do the parks then, see the animals?' the man in the hotel bar said to me after I'd been a week or so in Nairobi.

'Well, maybe. If there's time.'

'What—come all this way and not see the animals? You must be out of your mind.'

Well, that was it—that, and the elephant on the bumper and the importance to the economy. I was going to have to take a closer look at it all. So I dropped the model farms and the new light industry and took a plane to Moshi, a small town several hundred miles south-east of Nairobi in Tanzania at the foot of Mount Kilimanjaro, having got an invitation to look at the College of African Wildlife Management there, which has its headquarters half-way up the slope. The College, long proposed in colonial times as an essential part of a scheme to teach Africans how to manage their wildlife—as game wardens, scouts, and park rangers—only got started five years ago.

Moshi, the little town below the College, was originally a German agricultural settlement and the road which winds steeply up from the town passes through green coffee plantations and lush farms, in a few cases still owned by the original settlers, with the mountain and its great collar of snow and cloud always in front of one, glistening through the trees which cover its middle slopes, like a promise or a threat—depending on how you look at it.

'It's like Clapham junction at this time of year as far as the climbers go,' Mr. Mence, the head of the Wildlife School, said to me as we drove up the mountain. 'And not always easy. A German died a few weeks ago at the top—of exposure. Hell of a job to get him down. The police weren't very interested.'

'And what's all this about finding the bones of a leopard way above the snowline,' I asked, remembering Hemingway's famous story *The Snows of Kilimanjaro*. 'Is it true no one knows what it was doing up that high?'

'Oh, I don't think so—probably chasing something or other. Smaller animals have been known to get up there, escaping from something. You know the mountain was a gift from Queen Victoria to the Kaiser in the last century,' he went on. 'That's why it's now in Tanzania now and not Kenya.'

Mr. Mence was a little prosaic about the whole thing, I thought. Still, to me the mountain looked suitably legendary and certainly it gave the College a marvellously dramatic setting. At 10,000 feet up the air is crisp as broken ice and when I was there the huge trees and bougainvillaea round the College were blowing their rusty purple leaves over the basketball and squash courts and over the roofs of the neat red-tiled bungalows and one had the impression of some splendid Swiss health resort in the late autumn.

The College is presently financed by the Tanzanian government and by the United Nations Development Programme, one of the really effective parts of the U.N., and it was pleasant, after the endless argy-bargy of the General Assembly, to come across another and so different an aspect of United Nations work —one which was really going to have an impact on African life.

What sort of people does the College hope to turn out—what does a Game Warden actually *do*, I wondered. I'd imagined a sort of Jack Hawkins figure in an old bush hat and a land rover always chasing poachers. But it seems there's a little more to it than that.

'He has to know his law,' Mr. Mence said. 'His court procedure—when he catches the poachers. And then he's in charge of government trophies, shot ivory and so on, often of great value. So he must be completely reliable. Of course he'd have to track a man-eating lion—and there *is* that sort of drama. But there's a good deal more to the job than just bravery.'

Of course, too, the warden goes on safari . . . Safari is really a much over-worked word in English. In Swahili it means simply a journey, any sort of a decent journey, round the mountain to see your uncle or a trip to Nairobi for your son's wedding. But for us unfortunately it's come to mean simply getting the animals properly between your sights, in tailored bush jackets with custom-made express rifles: it's privilege, money and excitement—in full technicolour with a bronzed professional hunter and six crates of whisky. I liked the idea vaguely, as one does ideas which one will never be able to afford. In fact, I was very lucky. The students at the College were going out on safari —just to look at the game—a few days after I got there, to Tsavo National Park, one of the biggest game reserves in Africa, about half the size of Wales, and I was able to go along with them

These were first-year students, few of whom had any experience of wild animals, let alone stalking them—unarmed, on foot as we were going to do—through the bush. I wondered if this was really wise. It was the sort of nervous question people ask who've been reared on the Hollywood idea that any animal outside a zoo will go for you at the slightest opportunity. Frank Poppleton, previously Warden at Queen Elizabeth National Park in Uganda and now one of the College instructors, was marvellously sang froid about this—a tall, bronzed, fair-haired man, better than Jack Hawkins, in a bush hat and land rover.

'There is an element of danger,' he said. 'But providing you don't overstep the mark, you get away with it. We know these animals fairly well and there are certain symptoms. For instance, if you are close to an animal, particularly an elephant, his eyes are very exposed and his eyelids are open and his eyes are showing and staring, glaring, his tail comes up into a sort of knot, and his trunk comes in close to his body—well, then you're in for trouble. But if he feeds docilely and he hears you, looks at you, and then wanders off feeding—well you're all right. We couldn't do this sort of thing in an area where elephant had been hunted a lot. Only in a National Park. One of the animals which is reckoned to be rather stupid but which in fact is incredibly dangerous is the hippopotamus. On one occasion, in Uganda, I was out with my wife and we were walking up the banks of the Nile, and a hippo came out and charged us at sort of zero feet. And we stood our ground simply because we were completely paralysed. And this animal came for us, his mouth moving up and down, as it very often does when they are perturbed, and these great big teeth were showing—well, it came hard, and I screamed at the thing, and I had a walking stick and I slammed it across the snout. Now I'm absolutely certain that had we run the results would have been disastrous. The fact is that if you stand up to these animals and face them, most of the big game, nine times out of ten they'll break.'

That's the stuff, I thought. And I hoped there'd be lots of walking sticks with us on the journey. This trip to Tsavo wasn't, of course, the traditional sort of big game-hunting safari. There were no guns, no shower baths hooked up under the acacia trees, no spring mattresses or dry martinis and no Ava Gardners—and we camped each night, not in tents, but in a ruined mining village that had closed up years before, at the edge of the park, far from where the tourists were allowed to go. And in a way, this staying in the crumbling manager's house with the students camping out in the old labour lines, was far more creepy and strange than tents under the stars. There was no electricity, yet the bulbs and electric fires had never been taken away and I found an old hair-dryer in a cupboard. There were damp, battered copies of *Punch* and *Country Life* for 1947 in the pantry and a broken lavatory which flushed mysteriously in the middle of the night as if the manager had suddenly returned. The annexe to the house had been the communities clubroom and there was a last notice pinned carefully on the wall above the rotten billiard table: 'Staff are reminded that glasses should not be placed on the cloth and that Bar credit has been suspended'.

In the evenings, when it got cold and pitch dark within half an hour, great blocks of cedar from a ruined tree in the garden roared in the living-room grate, the petrol lamps hissed like snakes as they were pumped up in the kitchen and people chatted and laughed over their beers before dinner.

There was no question—this was the life all right. But how

did you get into it? One of the instructors was Pat Hemingway, Ernest's son—and very like an early version of his father. We opened some more beer. He talked; I listened.

'I'm sure that the greatest influence in my coming to Africa must have been my father. He first came to Africa when I must have been about four years old, so this obviously didn't make much impression on me at the time. But I do remember when I was about seven, eight years old, listening to the stories about that first trip of his—what a marvellous country Africa was: you woke up in the morning and there was ice in the wash basin and so forth; snow on the equator, all the animals like it used to be in the American West fifty, sixty years before. And I had the chance to do a lot of shooting when I was a child and I think anyone who has been brought up as a hunter—well, it's the sort of dream of hunters to come to Africa. That's probably the original motive that got me to come. I won't say it's what sustained me once I got here!'

For the next week we were out every morning at the absolute crack of dawn—looking for the animals. Elephant particularly. Tsavo probably has the largest concentration of them anywhere in East Africa, about 22,000 it's thought. The method was always the same: someone would see a few lone bulls or a breeding herd on the horizon and we'd swerve off after them across the bush, sometimes stopping half a mile or so down wind of them in the lorry and then going after them on foot: at other times just getting as close to them as possible in the lorry and sitting tight.

The purpose, in each case, was to give the students confidence in dealing with the animals close to. It seemed to me the most hair-raising pursuit and before the end of the week I was about to ask if I could stay behind in camp. But by then we were out looking for far less dangerous beasts, it seemed to me—lion and rhino, where we stayed firmly put in the lorry and some distance away from them. But the elephants I came to mistrust infinitely. Bull herds were perfectly innocuous. They continued to browse as we approached, taking no notice of us at all. Breeding herds were quite different. At the first sound of the lorry they would mass round in circles—the totos, the baby elephants, in the middle—and then face us. At about a hundred yards from them we usually stopped and by then the leading two or three females would be coming for us, trunks raised and swirling, ears flapping, at a fast trot in a cloud of dust and with the most fearful trumpetings. One elephant is large enough while standing absolutely still, as they do in zoos. A crowd of them coming for you at twenty miles an hour in open country is something not to be contemplated for long. The first time it happened with us the students in the back of the lorry bolted over the sides and disappeared into the bush. I would have done the same except that I was in the front seat at the time, hemmed in on one side by an awkward door handle and on the other by Mr. Mence, as calm as if he were confronted by nothing more than a herd of cows. When they got to within fifty yards of us he revved the engine violently several times and all the elephants stopped at once—still carrying on in the most dreadful manner, pawing the ground and shrieking, but at a dead halt.

'A demonstration charge,' he said. 'Revving the engine puts them off their stride. A real charge is quite different. Then they put down their trunks between their legs and their ears flat back—and that's when you get out fast.'

Later he gave the students a good ticking off for running away. 'If I'd had to pull out of here quickly you'd all have been left behind. That was stupid.'

'What would have happened?' I asked.

'Well, an elephant has an incredible sense of smell but he can't see much—just dark blurs beyond twenty yards or so. If there's a group of you on foot, and they're really charging, the thing to do is to separate and run in different directions. That confuses them and they'll stop—after a while. It's perfectly safe if you know what you're doing.'

And the students quickly learnt. Indeed they became quite fearlessly accustomed to these daily 'demonstrations' while I began to pray we wouldn't see another elephant on the horizon as we careered over the range.

Towards the end of the week we went down to Mzima Springs in the centre of the park. This is an incredibly green, Eden-like depression in the centre of the dry, dusty scrubland where the water gushes forth from a rock into a crystal-clear pool and here the hippos amble about in the depths, gliding over the stones at the bottom like great dark barrage balloons dancing. It was an extraordinary vision, since nearly always in Africa, as in zoos, the hippos are never so visible in their natural element, but usually quite out of sight, except for nose and ears, in murky water.

This was one of the main tourist attractions of the park and there must have been about fifty elderly Americans looking out over the pool when we arrived. Dead silence. Just a loud whirring noise. Every one of them had a movie camera and was hard at it. And one saw these people all over East Africa, sweating under the sun in their pork-pie straw hats, baseball caps and brightly coloured shirts; bedraggled and lost at sunset over a tomato juice in one of the game lodges: Americans of an older generation, as Osbert Lancaster drew them in the immediate post-war years. In some ways they were as interesting to watch as the animals themselves, or some of the African tribes with their extraordinary trinkets hanging from ears and lips and neck. For like them they were always festooned, falling over themselves, with cameras and tripods and immense, almost obscene, zoom and telescopic lenses. They 'saw' the animals all right, but not their background, the manner and place in which they lived—not their 'ecology' as the word is.

And here we are at that endlessly debated question of wildlife conservation in Africa: are all the animals dying out, really in danger of extinction—or what? No, it seemed to me, and far more importantly to several experts I spoke to. Several species, such as the elephant, are presently increasing at a dangerous rate in some areas. The real problem now is that of keeping a balance among the animals and, above all, of preserving their *total* environment.

'The important thing now,' Pat Hemingway told me, 'is to preserve *not* the individual animal, but the *way of life* of the animal. Individual animals come and go but the environment stays and this is what we must preserve. There are many cases where misguided people have preserved the individual animals and allowed them to increase to such an extent that they create what could be called an animal slum—where no individual animal any longer enjoys any personal freedom or has enough to eat.'

Among other threats to the animals, poaching remains. And with areas as big as these National Parks and game reserves it's unlikely ever to be entirely stamped out. But it's not the comprehensive threat it was in the past. Indeed the idea that the wildlife in East Africa would suffer as a result of independence coming to Kenya, Uganda and Tanzania has not been realized. Just the opposite. With the vastly increased revenue from tourists and the possibility, at least, of cropping certain wild animals for food, game laws have never been more vigorously or widely enforced.

Three lionesses stalking some waterbuck in the early morning light by the river—moving onto them, each from a different direction, pushing them back towards the water as the buck sensed something wrong, the yellow shapes sliding from bush to bush, crawling, right down, hardly a foot above the ground. Stopping suddenly, moving on—and then one of them rising too soon for the kill, making a hopeless dash behind a clatter of hooves as the waterbuck got away along the bank. Three old bull elephants, huge, with yellowing tusks, nursing a small buffalo that had been separated from its herd and was partially blind—nudging it away from the lorry, prodding it delicately out from between their feet. A rhino charging our empty lorry viciously, repeatedly one afternoon when we got back from looking at a waterhole: all this was one sort of safari—a journey to *look* at the animals. But of course there are the other sort still too—the journeys to shoot them. Yet as Pat Hemingway told me, there's not such a difference between killing an animal and conserving it: the two are simply a part of a larger ebb and flow of life in the bush.

'Wildlife is a "renewable resource" as the jargon puts it. The average life of an antelope in the wild is about four years. They are constantly meeting with accidents, being eaten by lions, wild dogs—they can have their necks broken by a cheetah. They can get themselves stuck between two trees and die of starvation. So really being shot is not one of the worst things that can happen to them. I think the principal thing to get across to people who don't believe in this sort of hunting is that we are only able to exist on earth because things die. We are all made out of a few simple substances and we are allowed to use these for a certain length of time—and then we have to step aside and allow someone else to use them. And it's only people who have not looked the natural world clearly in the face who cannot accept the idea of death in the wild—through hunting, which is only one among many unnatural ends which animals meet with. Life builds up combinations of things and death destroys them so that new combinations can be built. But neither process can exist without the other.'

Some people told me that the professional hunters were dying out in East Africa, that they were a colonial relic and would have disappeared completely within the next ten years or so. Others said just the opposite.

'This is one job they can't Africanize,' one of them said to me at the Long Bar of the New Stanley hotel in Nairobi, their traditional meeting place. 'It's a lot more than just banging your way through a licence list, you know. Takes more than a year or two to learn—and then the client wants chatter and bridge and stories after dark, as well as the trophies. I feel quite secure.'

He's probably right. Big game hunting is a multi-million industry in East Africa and although there are several African professional hunters, the financial return to the governments there is far too important for them to consider any drastic changes in the presently almost entirely European set-up.

In the mid-Thirties Ernest Hemingway described professional hunters as men who 'worked three months of the year and drank for the other twelve'. Only a suspicion of this sort of casual high-life is left today. They've not quite exchanged their bush jackets for brief cases, it's true. But the financial rewards among the top thirty or so hunters is now so great, and the safari work itself so intense, that there is little time to talk about it all in bars. Many of the hunters have smart secretaries and gleaming offices in Nairobi and make trips to the States, like Savile Row tailors, to organize their clients beforehand. Still, when they do come back to Nairobi after a month in the bush, they do still sometimes drop by at the Long Bar. And then, amidst the general uproar and smoky brashness of the place, over mugs of beer and great steaks, they come more into line with the old idea one has had of the professional hunter, of the tough, rather mysterious figure, moving through the empty spaces with his gun: a sort of Shane of the bush who stalks the lion instead of the bad man.

I met Major Douglas Collins in the New Stanley one morning —among the most experienced hunters in East Africa, he's been at it for nearly thirty years—and asked him if there was any real substance in these romantic rumours.

'No. I'd say not. Forty years ago it was an honourable, a romantic profession. Now it's much more a business. Take the case of Denys Finch-Hatton who was killed out here before the war, flying his own little plane. Well, he was a poet, a classical Greek scholar, connoisseur of champagne. I'm told he could have been prime minister of England. None of his sort about these days.'

'It's rather a rat race now?'

'Very much so.'

Another hunter, Mohamed Iqbal—known everywhere as 'Bali' and a huge great jolly bear of a man—is a Pakistani and I asked him if these safaris were really like a Boy Scouts' outing, with caviar and champagne instead of bacon and eggs.

'Nothing like that at all, you know. We start our day at 4.30 a.m. And, by God, by the time I see that camp light, coming back about eight or nine o'clock at night, I think—first class, my dinner, a couple of whiskies and then bed. But then you have to sit around with this dude and talk to him until eleven. You know, in simple words, this is not hunting anymore—you're a nursemaid on safari, where you have to put them into bed too.'

Well, since I certainly couldn't afford a real hunting safari, I ordered some more beer for Douglas and Mohamed and asked them to take me on an imaginary one. Lion I said I was after. And we've just got to our hunting block. What happens next?

'If you're hunting in an area where you can bait,' Douglas said, 'and you've got the lion feeding on your bait—a zebra hung up in a tree we'll say—well, you have to be in the blind before dawn to catch him there. So I'm up at four or half-past on my safaris. You might come back for lunch, usually take a lunch box with you. Back at night, a bath, a couple of drinks—I never have more than two drinks on safari—then dinner. Then, with a talkative type, you have to entertain him, keep him amused, and you're very lucky to get to bed by eleven. And this goes on every day for thirty days you must remember. No Saturdays or Sundays off or anything like that.'

What sort of people were these 'clients' I wondered?—the elderly, unshaven, crew-cut men in expensive mackintoshes whom I'd see crowding Nairobi airport after the rains, just off the big jets with their armoury of guns sheathed in long black leather bags as casually as golf clubs. I'd had the image of people in the grip of a particularly unsporting obsession: to slaughter as much game as possible in the shortest and most comfortable period of time.

'Well, no. Normally no,' Douglas said. That can happen—the odd client who uses his game licence like he might use a menu at dinner. If you get a person like that you just have to be tough with them, show them the Kenya Game Ordinances—and control him.'

And were these clients always such competent sportsmen? Could all of them shoot as well as they thought they could? Or did the hunter—as I'd heard—sometimes have to shoot the animals for them.

Douglas came in fast here. 'Personally I hate anything being wounded. I get sick inside until the animal is dead. So if a client isn't a good shot—say it's an elephant—I always shoot immediately afterwards. And he's so tensed up that he doesn't know. He might say afterwards, "Well, you didn't shoot, did you?" And I say, "Certainly not." But that's how I get round it.'

And what about the evenings, I asked—what to do then?

'My technique was to do as much as possible during the daytime, so that when we got home no one wanted to discuss anything, just wanted to go to bed. This worked most of the time. Though every once in a while you had marvellous luck—you got somebody who came out on safari just to play cards. He wasn't really anxious about the hunting, as long as he had his little bit of outdoor life, and then came home early in the evening. Because the main event of the day was getting down to bridge. And usually these people came out in groups of four good players. They didn't want to run the risk of not being able to find another good bridge player on safari.'

One thing that puzzled me was that although almost all the professional hunters were English, none of them I met had ever taken out an English client. Douglas had an immediate explanation for this.

'At the turn of the century, the bewhiskered Victorian gentry —if they happened to have an unhappy love-affair—they would come out and take it out of the wretched lion and elephant and that sort of thing. I assume in England now there are probably no unhappy love-affairs. The welfare state—all that sort of thing taken care of. I would like to say—being a Kenyan citizen now, but born in Sherwood Forest—I would like very much to have your Prime Minister out on safari. I think he would make splendid lion bait.'

I ordered some more beer.

'What about these old films and books—the inevitable moment on safari when someone gets trampled on by an elephant or mauled by a lion? Usually Stewart Granger or Anthony Steel.'

'In my opinion there's no danger to the client whatsoever. Say you take him out to a lion, he shoots, he wounds it. Well, I'll "tut-tut" and say that's bad luck, old dear. Now you go back to the hunting car, have a cigarette, and I'll finish it off. No danger to the client whatsoever. That's why we get so well paid. All the danger descends on the steel-brained head of the white hunter—I beg your pardon—the professional hunter.'

'Do many of them in fact get killed?' I asked.

'Oh, yes. We had a very sad loss last year. One of our better lion hunters got mixed up with a lion and he was killed.'

'He wasn't killed by a lion,' Bali put in judiciously. 'He was shot dead by one of his inexperienced gun-bearers who let go and hit him right smack behind and killed him instantly.'

However, as far as the client is concerned this sort of trophy safari all seemed a little too prepared, too comfortable, to *un*-dangerous; not at all the callous slaughter I'd imagined, but simply an exclusive titillation for the jaded rich, a cossetted journey for something to put on the drawing-room floor or hang in the study. It wasn't really an adventure at all. But whatever we think of the morality of it, we may in any case be seeing the last of these large-scale, luxury trophy safaris.

'It's no profession for a youngster,' Dougie Collins said. 'It's a dying profession. It might last another ten years or so. Most clients, out on a month's safari, can still get four or five of the big five—that is: lion, leopard, buffalo, rhino or elephant. But in a few years' time, with the population explosion, you'll get a clash between animals and humans, and it cannot last.'

Still, it's going full blast at the moment and before I left Nairobi I met Liam Lynn, one of the youngest professional hunters in East Africa, who was going out next morning on quite a different sort of safari, with quite a different sort of client: a safari very much in the old style, as it first was in Africa before the lorry and the land rover took all the sweat out of it. The client was John Heminway—no relation of the Heming-ways—an American in his twenties, a writer and traveller in

Africa. We were in the Norfolk bar this time, at the top of the town, on the terrace, looking at one of the rickshaws preserved there in the forecourt, the common means of transport for the elderly Raj of the place fifty years before. Heminway looked at the vehicle dismissively, sipped his lager and began to ruminate. It was warm and very dark outside, except for the huge constellations above us, the endless glittering pin-pricks of light which fall over these high plainlands each dusk.

'Tomorrow we're off on this safari to the Northern Frontier District,' John said. 'It's an area where the hunting must be done by horse and camel. It adds a real dimension of excitement to the sport of hunting, and one more dimension to the idea of being in the bush. That's my only reason for going out there. We drive first to a place called Marilal and we establish a base camp near there. And then on we don't use cars anymore. We are entirely dependent on four horses and six camels which will carry our gear. And we'll set off on week long forays into the bush, tracking the elephant.'

Talking to Heminway, as he got going, I began to see something of the unique attractions of hunting, of being, in Africa— the mystique of the whole thing if you like, which the other Hemingway, Karen Blixen, Gerald Hanley and others have written so much about. It's obviously still a powerful spell.

'I'm really after one animal. And that's an elephant. The elephant, I think, is one of the noblest creatures that exist in Africa and it is the final and greatest hunt to go after this mammoth creature. The elephant symbolizes the great chase and to do it by chasing after it in a land rover would seem to defeat the purpose of my coming to Africa. I'm going after this elephant in a rather unorthodox fashion—because it's giving the elephant more of a chance. But I think more than that, we are going to spend most of the time stalking the animal. Whether we shoot the animal or not is going to be inconsequential. It's a stalk— for better or worse.'

Well, I don't know whether he got his elephant or not. But it certainly seemed a more appropriate way of going about it than going with shower baths, spring mattresses and dry martinis. Liam Lynn, the hunter he was going with, was perfectly happy about the future of the whole business.

'When I started professional hunting in 1956 friends said it

would only last a couple of years. But it's still going strong.
Sometimes one's inclined to get depressed. I think I should be
doing something more constructive. The world is divided into
producers and non-producers and sometimes I feel I'm a non-
producer. However, I've found from my experience that a good,
a successful safari, to people who've dreamt and lived and
planned it for years, can be one of the most wonderful things of
their life. And I feel that if I can contribute to making the
vacation of a lifetime for somebody then I *am* producing.'

'I think,' John Heminway went on, 'that the bush—the idea
in philosophical terms—is a concept which is dying. And I think
every human being, somewhere in their lives, longs for something untarnished. This is what the fabulously successful,
urbane type who makes up most safaris yearns for. And this is
what I, far humbler than they, yearn for. When I'm fifty I'll
want it even more, I think. And I hope at that point in my life
there will still be an Africa to come to.'

Well, so much for the mystique of hunting and of the wildlife in general in East Africa. The mystique certainly exists, as
strong as ever. And perhaps it's not so much of a mystery if one
makes the effort to get properly involved as John Heminway
was doing. The excitement of the place really comes from that,
from really *being*, living in the country, for longer than a
package tour or a photo safari—in seeing the place as a totality
and not, as a tourist, seeing it all through a camera, or as the
trophy hunter who sees only the ivory at the end of a rifle.

'A country,' Ernest Hemingway wrote about Africa thirty
years ago,' 'was made to be as we found it. We are the intruders
and after we are dead we may have ruined it but it will still be
there.'

The thing about East Africa is that it *is* still there—the
hundred-mile views, the rain forests, the green hills, snow on the
equator, vast spaces of empty land and many of the animals,
just as they were, not ruined at all. I think Hemingway was
being over-pessimistic, indeed that the whole recent panic about
the destruction of the land and the wildlife in East Africa has
been slightly overdone. Of course there are not the vast herds
roaming freely over the country as there were at the turn of the
century. But the animals that are left are being preserved—and
they are being shot, competently, carefully now in both cases.

After the ravages of the last fifty years another balance, rational rather than simply natural, is coming about. And the problem in this age of the frenzied package tour, the Hollywood exaggerations and the sentimental animal books, is what sort of balance we can achieve, in thinking of the animals, in looking at them.

2

A Rose in the Desert

[May 1971]

It was late afternoon. We were sitting at the bar of the Ras Hotel, Addis Ababa—myself and this Ethiopian who had the air of a Special Branch man. I'd just arrived in Ethiopia and my friend, as it turned out, did work for the police. He was a very literate policeman and we'd had seven drinks.

'This is one of the hotels your English writer stayed at,' he was saying. 'Mr. Waugh—I think his name was—back in the 'Thirties.'

'*Scoop*, was it—or *Black Mischief*?'

'I'm not sure—one of his African novels.'

'Are you really a policeman?'

'Of course not.'

'Why did you say you were then?'

'I didn't.'

I leant across and tapped a bulge just beneath his breast pocket.

'What's that then?'

'All Ethiopians are armed. It can still be quite dangerous here.'

He looked at me seriously, and I looked at the cockroaches clambering over the bar telephone and along the counter and up the whisky bottle which served as a light. They would get to the top of the fly-smeared yellow shade and then they'd stumble, one by one, into the bulb with a slight hissing noise. All Ethiopians are armed, I thought, and know about Evelyn Waugh. A potentially explosive situation and I'd better be careful in my researches about the place.

I ordered another drink and the barman produced a glistening bottle of St. George's lager, with a picture of the saint and the dragon locked in mortal combat on the label. Then suddenly my friend finished off his beer in one long draught and put the glass down with a thump. Two other gentlemen in bulky jackets had just arrived in the doorway.

'Well, we must meet again—this evening perhaps. My name is George, like the saint on the lager bottle,' he said, patting me on the shoulder. 'And I *know* yours.' And George went out into the evening, in his hand-made brogues and distinguished worsted. He was a very *un*-plain-clothes man.

Indeed, like a number of metropolitan Ethiopians he was inordinately grand and in touch with affairs way beyond his own country. And perhaps because of the Emperor's long exile in England before the war, at a South Coast resort, there was about him too, as with the others, a decidedly Edwardian flavour—a confident, graceful, rather studied attitude, as if he were seriously thinking of cracking a bottle of Cockburn's '37 with one.

The thing about Addis Ababa is that it gives one no sense of being in a capital city at all. It's really a succession of small, half-built towns with lots of villages and even fields in between, and this is rather nice. There is a complete haphazardness about the place: nothing coheres in any direction. It's an utterly engrossing collection of concrete and mud and tarmac and open drains. It seemed to me that the large piazza outside my hotel with its old-fashioned buildings and colonnades, its open-air cafés and airline offices, must be somewhere near the centre of things. But I thought I'd just check with the doorman.

'Is this the downtown area?' I'd seen a notice saying so on the way in from the airport.

'No,' he said. 'Up Churchill Avenue. At the top, where the cinema is. That's the downtown.'

'That's the main part of the town, is it?'

'No. That's where the cinema is. That's one downtown. There's another downtown by the university and the biggest downtown is up by the palace on that hill. You need a taxi?'

I decided to walk. Churchill Avenue is several miles long, allows for traffic coming in two directions and has a policeman with a large stick for controlling both cars and animals at the crossroads half-way up. It was obviously planned as a boulevard in the very grandest manner to link two of the larger parts of the town together. It does, in fact, link them—over a series of cavernous potholes and by means of little taxis which you use just like a bus, flagging them down and hopping in if they're going in your direction and there's room. But the intended grand design seems to have been delayed somewhat.

Most of the avenue is bounded by small, tin-roofed houses and shops, one-storeyed and very wobbly, tightly packed together like a row of drunks trying to stand up. Among them are a great many funeral parlours with elaborate, highly coloured, pop-art designs all over the coffins in the windows. These express religious, and other less sacred, intentions for the afterlife of the loved one, done in the very decorative Amharic script.

At the end of the avenue I found myself, without question, in one of the downtown areas. There was another piazza—only half complete and built on two sides round what looked like a village green—there was the cinema, a Greek bookshop with hundreds of old copies of the *News of the World*, and an excellent Italian restaurant whose only disadvantage lay in that it had as many rooms to eat *in* as there were tables to eat *from*, so that one ate in particularly isolated splendour and had to get up and call down the corridor for the next course.

Off the avenue—indeed off any of the several avenues of the city—is another matter completely: here one might have arrived in the middle of some raucous medieval carnival. The cobbled tracks run off into mere footpaths: steep, rutted gullies—streams in the rainy season—without direction, which thread their way among precariously-situated mud huts, each of which offers both drink and women in vast quantities. There is a great deal of shouting and much music—or it may have been the same thing —and everywhere green lights, above all the doorways, which puzzled me until I learnt afterwards that an edict had gone out at the time of Queen Elizabeth's visit that there were to be no more red lights in the city.

These back alleys have an air of incredible liveliness, with rough, friendly countrymen dressed in a sort of mini-toga and canvas jodhpurs—which is almost the national dress of the country—stumbling in and out of doorways and brandishing heavy sticks at the night. And other vague, elderly figures with long Byzantine faces and huge almond eyes, waving lanterns about and apparently offering to show you something or take you somewhere. I had some tedj in one of these bars and very nearly needed their assistance afterwards. Tedj, the national drink, is a kind of mead, sweet and musky and rather nice: it's one of those innocuous-tasting drinks which it's difficult to decide if you really like or not until you've had too much, and then it's of no importance what you think of it.

When I got back to the hotel that evening everyone was there, sure enough, except my friend George. Instead, I got talking to Afework, a local photographer, who was off to take some shots of a government project down the Awash valley—a river which runs off the 8,000-foot plateau where Addis lies and into the steamy lowlands towards the Red Sea.

'A project among the Danakil tribe,' he said rather warily, I thought.

'Who are they?'

'Rather a wild people, I'm afraid. Nomadic, obstinate, lazy and much given to fighting, especially now, after the rains. But interesting, certainly interesting. There's a spare seat on the plane, I believe, if you'd like to take a look at them.' I arranged to meet Afework two days later at the airport.

I suppose most people who get themselves to wild, remote countries hope to see something wild and remote in the way of people when they get there—something really untamed and not the usual drum-thumping and dancing which is laid on for the tourists. One hopes against hope, for little of this is left in Africa. However, from what Afework had said, perhaps this trip might be different: vast areas of Ethiopia were still utterly remote, unapproachable, unmapped, and one-way journeys into these places were still quite common.

The highland Ethiopians—the proud Amharas who run the country from their lush green plateau—certainly look upon the Danakil, and indeed all the other lowlanders, with the greatest misgivings, and we took off in the little aircraft with everyone, except myself, fairly heavily armed. Flying off this central plateau, especially after the long rains, is a startling experience. For the first half-hour east of Addis we were never more than five hundred feet or so above the ground, flying over a green and yellow chequerboard of fields and wild flowers, a marvellously fresh-coloured landscape, dotted with groves of eucalyptus trees, thatched huts and sleek herds of animals. A farmer on a white horse trotted along beneath us, one of the 'Big Men', as they're called in the country, his solar topee bobbing up and down, toga flapping out behind him, and followed by his retinue of servants chasing along after him on foot. In the distance, to our left above Addis, was a line of purple hills with small, pale blue lakes in between, glistening in the clear morning light—a light and a landscape amazingly like that of the Scottish Highlands or the West of Ireland.

And then it came to an end, this pastoral idyll, as sharply and dramatically as a cliff plunging into the sea. The land falls sheer away, for thousands of feet, into a shimmering haze of dust and heat and the yellow light of the desert, and the only movement left in this desolate landscape was the once tumbling, frothy river now circling slowly round in the sands far beneath us.

The river, in fact, was the reason for our trip. The Ethiopian government, together with the United Nations Development Programme—an arm of the UN which is helping to pay for hundreds of various agricultural projects all over the developing world—have started a scheme here to settle the nomadic Danakil. Because of the ready supply of water and the dry climate the area is ideal for growing cotton. Danakil, their spears actually beaten into ploughshares, were to become farmers and hurried into the twentieth century in a cloud of insecticide.

It was stiflingly hot after we landed on the cracked, sandy soil and the Danakil had all rushed out from their low grass huts to see us. The older men of the settlement stood a little apart, their women behind them, but the children—the child brides and the boys—clustered around the plane in a frenzy. 'They want to be the ones to guard it,' the pilot said. 'It's a great privilege to guard the bird. It's a bird to them, of course.' They were wild-looking certainly: the men naked except for a loin-cloth, a few festooned with bandoliers of brass cartridges and carrying ancient Italian rifles, and the others with tall spears and sharply curved, double-edged Arab daggers; the women just with dark cotton skirts—no ornaments, nothing else—a dusky, grey-hued skin, wiry hair built up around their heads like a cloche hat and flashing, laughing eyes. Attractive. Arab far more than African, wild perhaps, but not in the least savage. They were curious about us, but reserved as well.

'We're about seventy miles from the nearest road out here and the river isn't navigable,' Mr. Levy, the UN project supervisor, told me as we drove to the camp which he and the other two Israeli members of the team had built for themselves in a clearing beneath a few trees by the river. 'We were probably the first Europeans many of them had ever seen.'

The camp was rather comfortable for somewhere seventy miles from nowhere. They'd piped up water from the river, had flush lavatories and a shower which hooked up under an acacia tree. There were two large tin buildings—one for sleeping in, the other a kitchen, dining-room and storeroom which had an immense paraffin refrigerator crammed tight with lemons, tangerines and large frozen hunks of dark red meat. 'Wild boar,' said Mr. Levy as he mixed us an iced drink. 'Very good— and sometimes there's antelope too, quite a bit of shooting round here in fact.' I noticed several shotguns in a corner of the living-room, a copy of *The Ginger Man* poking out from beneath a stack of agricultural books and pamphlets and a two-way radio on a desk. Enough to pass the long evenings, I thought. But what about the fierce Danakil?—hardly enough to keep them off if they got upset.

'No, we get along fine with them,' Mr. Levy said, 'as long as we don't get in their way when they're having one of their set-to's. The Isa—a much more aggressive tribe from over the hill there—come down in the dry season and try to push the Danakil off their grazing lands, which are better near the river. Then there's trouble. Half a mile away one night last week the two tribes had a real go at it—twenty-six dead next morning. We stayed indoors.'

That afternoon we went down to look at the Danakil, very peacefully working their cotton plots—the small green plants, several months old now, pushing their way up through the muddy, constantly watered soil—and the whole green and black 150 acres, cut out from the immense dusty plain as neatly as a new carpet, was very impressive.

'A rose blooms in the desert,' I turned to Mr. Levy.

'I think you could say that.' He smiled.

Towards the river the Danakil had their settlement of small huts—like igloos, about four feet high, just a pile of grass mats laid over a skeleton of bent sticks, with a door about as big as a foxhole, so that the whole lot can be rolled up and carried about with them on their camels. I crawled inside one of them and in the half-light could just make out a rather well-constructed wooden bed—rather like the beds of the ancient Pharaohs in the

Cairo museum—raised a few inches above the ground, with strips of criss-crossed animal hides as springing. And in one corner a few shallow wooden bowls and a pigskin of water. Nothing else, but distinctly cosy and surprisingly cool after the fierce glare outside.

'Of course, the first thing they want when they get a return on their cotton crop next year is a house,' Mr. Levy said. 'Just a tin hut, which won't be half as cool. Then furniture, clothes, schools, clinics, transistors—the lot. They're very keen to settle down—many more people are putting in for plots here than we've room for at the moment. And it's understandable. They've never had much of a life around here really, what with the Isa, the droughts, the diseases. We try as much as possible not to alter their tribal structures and so on. But of course it's going to be a big change for them. It's inevitable—not because we want it that way, but because *they* do.'

3

The Dancing Waiters

[April 1971]

Malawi in this century has had a habit of getting pushed slightly off the map by its much larger and more politically prominent neighbours, Zambia and Rhodesia, with whom until recently it was so unsuccessfully federated. And before then, in the heyday of British colonialism in Africa, when it was just the protectorate of Nyasaland, it was still rather an out-of-the-way backwater: a charming highland resort, not a lot bigger than Ireland, where people from South Africa and the Rhodesias came to spend their holidays by the lake—the long, dramatic slit in the land which David Livingstone first came across in 1859. Today, too, since Malawi has opened diplomatic relations with South Africa, the country is again very much on its own among the new African nations.

One surprising thing about it is that in a decade which has seen the British packed up and put away all over Africa, they are still to be found in Malawi: many retired people, many more in the Civil Service—about three-quarters of which is still British —and a steady intake of new people from Britain and elsewhere. Some of these people are the old-style colonial public servants who, though they no longer actually run the country, still play a large part in implementing government policy and who live in Malawi in much the same way as they've always done. There is just a suspicion of Tunbridge Wells or Cheltenham about the place.

Malawi, in part, is a little, animated museum of all those genteel colonial comforts and attitudes that one had thought utterly vanished along with the more brutish, ponderous aspects of that rule. A little austere, well-intentioned, still totally confident of their place in the world, the mood among the British in Malawi seems to have set somewhere around the summer of 1947. Indeed, the only books in the drawing-room of the government hostel in Zomba, where I spent my first night, was a

British-South African commercial almanac for that same year advertising various facilities in connection with King George VI's visit to the Union, and a musty copy of *Wisden* for 1948 recounting Denis Compton's prodigious cricketing feats the previous season.

In some ways, this poking around a boxroom of Imperial adventure was completely engrossing; in others, it was fair hell. The food was never less than deplorably cooked: chops rigid in their own coagulated gravy, and the marvellous vegetables of the country stewed for hours in unsalted water which became the soup for the following day. And one found, too, in some of the British that one met, that unique English talent for remaining uninvolved: a complete lack of interest in where they were or what they were doing, a hardly animate condition from which only mention of Mr. Wilson's name could rouse them. But in most other ways being with these people was agreeable enough: cucumber sandwiches, tennis parties and gin and lime at the Gymkhana Club at six was rather the order of things.

Zomba, the capital, about 3,000 feet up in the Shire High-lands, is the Washington of Malawi. It is a tiny place, not more than 20,000 people, almost all of whom are involved in some way with the administration of the country, and it must be one of the most attractive towns in Africa. Built into the steep, thickly wooded sides of Zomba mountain which rises sheer above it, it's a complete garden city in miniature, with huge clumps of purple bougainvillaea and red fever trees everywhere you look. There are hardly any shops, no cinemas and no hotels: for all that one must go forty miles south to the bustling, very ugly commercial centre of Blantyre. Zomba remains very much as it was—a nineteenth-century hill station, a cool, unhurried place of leisurely decisions and brief, deeply scented twilights.

A hundred miles north of Zomba is the great lake, Lake Malawi, 350 miles long and one of the chief attractions of the country, since apart from its dramatic beauty it's one of the few stretches of water in Africa which is bilharzia-free, so that one can swim in it. The area around the lake was originally a tribal arcadia of Pygmies. It was overrun in the fourteenth century by the fierce Bantu from the north, who in turn were decimated by the Arab slavers from the coast—who themselves were then wiped out by the British towards the end of the last century.

Some of all these influences can be seen in the Malawi people today, but perhaps the hordes of conflicting missionaries who descended on the lake with the British have had the greatest impact on the country: Malawi, through the good Dr. Livingstone, was missionary-land *par excellence*. They got there earlier than in most other parts of Africa, and because of their fierce rivalries worked their flocks more intensively in the ways of God, multiplication and the alphabet, so that most Malawians had a head start in the ways of the world over the rest of Africa. Being restlessly shuttled between different civilizations continues even today. It is a poor country—the World Bank gives Malawi as having the lowest per capita income in the world— but it lives next door to the diamond and copper mines of South Africa and Zambia, so several hundred thousand Malawians have to move around for their work and only come back home for holidays or to settle down, like the Irish from Birmingham. And this mobility has given them—as it did the Irish—a waggish, voluble, self-confident, realistic nature not always apparent elsewhere in Africa.

I can remember very well the waiters in the government hostel in Zomba who not only served one at table but danced to and from the kitchen as well. There were half a dozen of them— rotund, moustachioed gentlemen, in grubby white suits and flapping plastic sandals—and they would literally dance, out from behind the wings, as it were, of the two serving screens at the end of the room. And some of the more confident would emerge in a sort of frenetic military ballet, the 'left turn' from the kitchen executed in a neat *pas de deux*, both feet off the ground, one arm clutching a pillar, the other high above their heads carrying a piece of welsh rabbit like a sacred offering. And on their return, if they met one of their colleagues, they'd skip neatly out of the way, both feet together, like children playing hopscotch. Nobody else in the room took the least notice of these extraordinary goings-on, preferring to bolt their food and get down to the Gymkhana Club for more acceptable diversions —cigarettes at a shilling for twenty, spirits not much more for a measure and a game of darts.

Fort Johnston, the little town at the foot of Lake Malawi, was one of those Imperial outposts which so often figured in Victorian adventure books when the writer wanted to show

something of the tough privations and responsibilities of life in
Her Majesty's Colonial Service. Physically at least, the little
place doesn't seem to have changed much: it's still rather like
something from a story in *Blackwood's Magazine* for 1895. The
large, mud-bricked, yellow-washed, tin-roofed houses, built for
the DC, the doctor and the Inspector of Police, are just as they
were and are used, even today, by the same sort of English
officials: a little sombre, with deep rotting verandas and overgrown gardens, the remains of crazy pavements and herbaceous
borders, they look out over the broad Shire River which drains
the lake with an emphatic self-importance, much at odds with
the small buildings of the settlement, until one remembers that
it was from here that Livingstone and the other missionaries set
off on their embattled discoveries about the lake, and from here,
too, in 1895, that Sir Harry Johnston, with a flotilla of gunboats
and 400 troops, embarked on his short campaign against the
Arab slavers which ended in their fearful slaughter at Mpata
near the northern shores. Fort Johnston, in fact, gateway to the
lake, was one of those remote linchpins of Empire—a crucial
link in the chain which brought knives and forks, policemen and
Bibles, and all the other blessings of civilization, from England
to the savage wastes beyond. Nothing of such moment centres
round the place today. The lake has long since been tamed, and
Fort Johnston has become a relic of the Victorian faith in the
commercial, military and apostolic perfectibility of man: a
sleepy, isolated fragment of Africa where the past has been
casually preserved simply because the present has no immediate
use for it.

There were no cars and few people to be seen as we rolled up
the one main street which led down to the river. It was a
beautifully spacious avenue with bougainvillaea and arched plane
trees overhead, the afternoon light filtering through, the neat
nineteenth-century colonial bungalows set back in a line from
the street, the police station with its flag and ancient field-gun
staring up into the trees, and at the end of the road, looking out
over the ferry where the slaves crossed over on their terrible
journey to the coast less than a hundred years ago, a splendid
neo-Gothic Cleopatra's Needle done in startling red brick and
gilt—a monument celebrating Queen Victoria's Diamond Jubilee
from the 'Grateful Citizens of Fort Johnston'.

Here I met Gilbert Lewis, the DC, who has been stationed at the lake on and off since the early 'Thirties, and later we went back to his splendid tin mansion and sat on the veranda over our whiskies until it got quite dark and the frogs began to croak. The ferry squeaked on its iron ropes as it was pulled to and fro across the water, and the people going back from their jobs in the town shouted and whistled and stamped their feet on the metal raft, and in the very far distance across the river to the east flames lit up the sky and drums started to beat. 'Bush fires,' Lewis said. 'And trouble perhaps. That's where it comes from— over the border.'

We had curry for supper, a huge propeller-like fan swirling round high above us, gently rustling a copy of last month's *Times* on the chintz sofa, and afterwards we talked about London. 'Do the shop assistants still wear morning suits in Fortnum and Mason? I read somewhere that a Canadian had taken the place over.' At midnight the DC's generator stopped and the few lights in the town went out. The frogs redoubled their fearful barrage.

The next morning we went down the Shire River to look at an irrigation project which the government had started, together with the United Nations Development Programme—a part of the UN which is involved in promoting various agricultural schemes all over the developing world. 'What's the project for?' I asked Mr. Merrit, the UN official who'd come with us. 'Don't things grow well enough around here as it is?' 'On the banks of the river, yes. But inland, where there's very little, things could grow there just as well, if there was water. The land could give much more than just food for the people: cash crops, exports—that's what we have in mind.' With a flap of its huge tail a crocodile suddenly propelled its way back into a papyrus swamp further on. The sandy banks and villages which we'd passed earlier were behind us now, and we were travelling between the dense foliage of trees and creepers which border this part of the upper river. Hornbills—tiny, awkward, prehistoric-looking birds, with large beady eyes and huge, brilliantly coloured beaks—flapped away from us; pairs of green cormorants swerved over the water, and crested cranes with their silver haloes peered at us remotely from out of the papyrus. At times we had to avoid swarms of tiny, mist-like flies in the middle of

the stream which can concentrate themselves sufficiently around
a person's face to suffocate him. Apart from the seasonal bush
fires which coloured the sky a dirty hazy blue for miles around,
we might have been half-way up the Amazon, a thousand miles
away from any ideas of cash crops and irrigation schemes. 'Ah
yes,' said Mr. Merrit, gazing wistfully at the thick papyrus
swamps, 'that would make good land, if you could clear it.
They're trying it out in Kenya. That may be the next thing.'

In several other important ways Malawi remains today a step
or two outside the current political consensus among the new
African nations. It has not attempted to Africanize every
government position just for the sake of doing so, admitting that
it will be some time before Malawians can run everything for
themselves. Malawi must, having no seaports, trade with and
through the governments of Mozambique, Rhodesia and South
Africa: manufactured goods must come from somewhere, two
of these countries are next door to Malawi, and half a million of
her four million citizens live there; it is simply as a matter of
realism and survival that they deal with them. And this is the
keynote among Malawians: realism, a certain canniness, and a
peculiar, delightful tendency towards the bizarre, as with the
dancing waiters: and never more in evidence than at the opening
of Parliament which I got back to Zomba just in time for next
day.

The Parliament building, looking over the Botanical Gardens,
was like a very grand, very modern village hall, with an entrance
much like a cinema without the box-office. I'd tried to get a seat
in the press gallery but was told I'd have to have a morning
suit, so instead I lined up behind a troup of Boy Scouts and some
very old women, opposite the red velvet podium where the
President, Dr. Banda, was going to review the Guard of Honour.
There was a great deal of anticipatory chuckling and scuffling
from the crowd, and people walked quite freely to and fro across
the processional route which led up the hill through the wilting
bougainvillaea which littered the road with a feathery blue and
white confetti. After a while three glittering figures appeared
at the Parliament entrance: the Attorney-General, a tiny figure
in a wig and gilded robe who at once started to advise a press
cameraman near him on suitable apertures for the day, and the
two heads of the Army and the Police—both British, very tall,

impeccably Sandhurst and Hendon, ramrod straight, with batons and white gloves and braided caps pulled right down over their eyes—who wandered rather uncertainly about, blinking in the strong light, their hands in that mandatory position which the English male automatically assumes during any sort of ceremony: locked firmly behind their backs.

A moment later Dr. Banda himself swept up the road in the most splendid open, maroon Rolls-Royce, covering the wildly cheering spectators in a cloud of purple bougainvillaea leaves. A small, avuncular man in dark glasses, top hat and superb morning suit, he walked carefully along the Guard of Honour and took the salute, the National Anthem and three ear-shattering rifle volleys with the greatest aplomb before moving indoors to outline government plans for the coming year.

When he got out again the claque of old ladies in their dazzling cotton-print frocks broke ranks through the Boy Scouts and surrounded his car and clapped and sang a very boisterous song, and then ran after him down the hill, with surprising energy. It wasn't until their voices had died away that I realized that the band, meanwhile, had been seeing the President off with its own bizarre regards—a ragged, high-spirited version of 'Colonel Bogey'. 'Did you see the President wink at the Attorney-General?' one of the ladies said afterwards, at the Gymkhana Club, and the point went the rounds that long afternoon over the champagne glasses. I'm sure he did. Dr. Banda is that sort of man, Malawi that sort of place.

4

Egyptian Diary

[August 1970]

At Cairo airport I am kept back for over an hour while they
decide to take all the last four issues of Jon Kimche's *New
Middle East Review* from me. The covers of this objective,
independent review are what upset them: brightly coloured,
child-like representations of Mid-East problems and events—and
most particularly the June issue which shows a Palestinian and
a Jew combining peacefully in a federated state. 'You make
jokes at us,' the customs officer keeps on shouting at me. A mob
of other passengers and officials gather round, and I actually do
hear the phrase 'Imperialist jackals!' from somewhere in the
background. I feel like the meat, not the jackal, and it does no
good at all when I point out that the June issue largely consists
of the full English text of President Nasser's May Day speech
and a very correct Soviet commentary by one of their Arab
experts. I am held while some senior official is sent for. It's now
2.30 a.m., the customs hall is acrid with a smell of sweat, like an
old laundry after a hard day's rummaging, and I am quite ready
to forgo my reading matter. But we must wait, everyone must
wait: it is the Egyptian pastime. I remember the advice of a
friend who once spent the night in a lock-up in Port Said, the
First Commandment of life by the Nile: 'Beware the toils of
Egyptian bureaucracy.' The great man himself arrives and falls
upon the *Review* with a serious, almost sensual pleasure—as
though, if the time shift were possible, he had been suddenly
confronted with *Playboy* and the key to the Rosetta Stone.
'Maleesh.' It's all right. I may go about my business—but not
before he goes carefully through the rest of my newspapers. All
foreign news is strictly classified here now, and I am a honey-
comb of forbidden, literate delights. 'And what is this? *Time,
Daily Telegraph, Times*? Ah no. I am afraid I cannot permit.'
The junior officer will get a cuffing for missing these goodies.
I am allowed to hang on to that day's *Evening Standard* and the

pull-out 'Money *Mail*' with a long article on hire-purchase holidays. I leave the entire customs force of the airport pressing studiously about their chief. The hall has become as silent as a library. *Maleesh*.

The weather is delightful—a brisk north wind from the sea which waves the heat away before it strikes further than one's brow—and the flame trees are in full red blinding bloom all along the Gezira corniche. The city itself is crumbling splendidly, not from bombs, just through lack of money and attention: the elaborate French-Levantine-style apartments on Kasr el Nil and Soliman Pasha with their excessive curly stucco, their decorative Rue de Rivoli arches, balconies and roof-balustrades are all rubbing away, splitting, eroding in the khamsin winds and the cracking sandy air. One feels that they will deteriorate just so far, like the second pyramid at Giza; the corners and firm shapes will disappear, but their essential form will then be preserved for ever in this hot-cupboard country. These turn-of-the-century Cairo buildings are just entering the ancient-monument business: stylish tyros in the art of sinking gracefully into the sands.

There is little in the city to suggest the vicious war on the Canal front eighty miles away: a blackout hardly different from the traditional dark fatigue of the Cairo grid, smudgy blue irises on car headlights, and blast walls—already taking on the venerable patina of tomb doors—in front of the more important buildings. There is plenty of food about, including, at this season, the excellent Egyptian mangoes, oranges, strawberries, lemons and even some slightly scabby apples. Bread, that dark bitter loaf like a deflated football bladder, is still, after fifty years, half a piastre, and other prices have remained remarkably stable. If food is the first essential for political stability the President must sleep easy. No, the only sign of the war is in the frustration and bad temper one senses, especially on the roads. The driving is unbelievably aggressive and every pedestrian has become a substitute Zionist. That—and this afternoon a young armless man in the street below my hotel: he was having a fit and literally tearing his clothes off piece by piece, wailing and shouting with hideous flair. He was eventually taken in hand by some portly loungers at a nearby café and given a glass of tea. Milky tea is the number one Egyptian restorative and he calmed down immediately. Otherwise one is mostly struck by the lack of tension and by the vast numbers of smartly-dressed, laconic young men meandering the evening streets. Why, with this continuing crisis, aren't they in the Army? And the point is brought home to one that there are 32 million Egyptians and 2½ million Israelis. Here there are people to spare indeed.

Mohammed Heikal has left *Al Ahram* as a hoped-for light in the murky corridors of the Ministry of National Guidance, but the building, his twelve-storey pyramid, remains an incredible and incongruous monument. A colossal edifice in aluminium and black marble, it rears up from the dusty mess of one of the inner slums, putting Thomson House and the *Mirror* building in a second division. It must be the only business address in Cairo where everything—and everyone—actually works, from the bilingual receptionists to the waiters on the twelfth-floor restaurant who have the hors d'oeuvres out on the table for you before you've reached your seat. I talk to a leader writer here, one of the élite 'page five' men, who explains the present political situation to me: it's a matter of a complex power game between two major and two minor players. He draws the state of play geometrically for me on a piece of substantial bonded paper, and within a minute he has reduced it to inky ribbons. 'Yes,' I say. And 'Of course, I see that'—and I barely see it at all. I trust nothing as vehement as his scribbling occurs. Though as far as the complexity is concerned, he is right: it is certainly a game of advanced chess being played out here—not dominoes.

The Egyptians have a passion for rumour, conspiracy and mis-information, for complicating and confusing any issue. Like the Irish they have been reared on suffering and occupation, and they delight in the by-products: in the clandestine approach to everything, in canny patience, the waiting game and the long way round. It means they find it difficult ever to agree among themselves but will always unite in telling a stranger what they think he'd like to hear. Both these devious capacities turn any sort of factual information here into clues to a three-dimensional crossword puzzle. Their other great art, of course, is constructive idling. Egyptians reach the heights when they are doing, or talk-ing about, nothing. In the Embassy Bar today, at the end of a furious argument between three racing men over which horse had won the Cromer Handicap at Gezira in 1908, I overheard the exact last words, followed by the stage directions, of *Godot*:

'Let's go,' one of them said. Nobody moved an inch. *Godot,* in fact, with its wordy, mis-shapen logic and dying humour, is a perfect handbook to Egyptian life.

No foreigner is allowed out of the city by car nowadays so for Alexandria I must take the air-conditioned, super-de-luxe express, and it is nearly all these things. But I'm drawn completely by the view as we charge along, ten feet above the Delta, in our aircraft seats. What an extraordinary sight it is this, monotonous and fascinating in just the same measure: a landscape which one thinks one knows well, either from experience or from illustrations, but which is always, in the event, boring and stimulating in a completely new way. Do they really still thresh the grain with the *norag,* that cumbersome Pharaonic sleigh, drawn by buffalo, circling over the sheaves like a snail, and winnow it by forking the gold from pile to pile so that the chaff blows away in the north summer wind from the sea? They do—and I had forgotten it as something from a very old geography book. And so, too, the irrigation had become a cliché until I actually saw it again: how the minute veins of water for every row are raised from the fingers of ditches, the arms of canals, the body of the Nile, by *sakias, shadufs* and Archimedes screws—by men and animals turning blindly in the same circles and with the same equipment for 5,000 years. How utterly complete, self-sufficient and recurring are the wherewithals. One is appalled, yet humbled, by the sameness and stability of this life, on an absolute billiard-table of alluvial green and yellow, under an even flatter cloudless lead-blue sky: a landscape and a life where there is no perspective, no variations or comparisons. How far away is that white cigar-shaped finger, swinging now behind the motionless crescent sail of a felucca? A mile or ten miles? And is it a missile or a minaret? In this world the questions have no meaning: it is neither possible nor necessary to answer them. It couldn't matter less.

Now the radar dishes turn ominously on Fort Kait Bay where the great lighthouse stood; the Yacht Club is closed and the western harbour is barred to what few foreigners—besides Russians and East Europeans—come here now. Alexandria has relapsed once more into a tattered provincial outpost: a military enclave, a beleaguered and slightly barbaric relic. The pulsing European city that it was for a century and a half hangs now by a thread as it undergoes one of its long sea changes. The forms are as yet everywhere the same: the Cecil Hotel with its forest of mirrors, the little cubby-hole back bar of the Criterion with its striking oriental murals, the bougainvillaea-shrouded villas behind the corniche at Stanley Bay and Sidi Bishr, the blue Scottish trams clanking from Ramleh to Victoria, the steeply-raked pre-war Peugeot taxis like affronted beetles. But the life styles that created these things are mysterious now as the habits of a lost tribe, the people themselves not even ghosts. It is not a question of having to make an effort to imagine that Justine, Cavafy or E. M. Forster walked this way. One makes that effort only to be faced with the certainty that there must have been some mistake. At the Bolanachi distillery behind the Greek hospital nearly all the output is earmarked for Russia, the cases piled high in the sweet, musty gloom. I look at the label on one of the brandy bottles. It has been specially printed in Russian and English. 'They insist on describing it as cognac,' my guide tells me, 'though in fact it's only brandy.' The abrasive Mediterranean spirit has disappeared, the Russians call the tune now. Yet perhaps at this moment some latter-day Chekhov has arrived in the city to take up a minor cultural appointment. He has already seen the fabulous carpet of spring flowers beyond Lake Mariout, had a beer in the Cecil, studied the ecology in the Rue Nebi Daniel, strolled about the city, through the scented windy afternoons, under a moist blue sky. He has the material for some sad new tale, another in the long line of expatriate stories, inspired by the sea-glitter of this empty watering place which is already pure fiction.

President Nasser addresses the National Assembly in Cairo. The building is like a perfect Victorian theatre: a horseshoe of raked benches surmounted by brass-railed, red-velvet balconies and boxes. A packed house waits in excellent humour for two hours; the arc lights crackle and a door on-stage opens. Enter the President and the young Libyan Premier, Colonel Gaddafi. The audience explodes. The long wait and the dramatic curtain-up have done the trick: it hardly matters now what they say. It is enough that the gods are here, alive and well. The President waits his cue while the Speaker declaims the Prologue. Physically he is a very large man, which his immaculate English tailoring does much to conceal, and there *is* a tigerish cast to the face. But essentially the expression is withdrawn, deprecating, even cautious—and when he speaks the voice is low-keyed, almost colourless. There is nothing of the rabble-rouser here, and none of the harsh rhetorical gutturals to which the language lends itself so well. He is talking about war, about blood and defiance, but he might, in his mild tones and quiet, rounded phrasing, be reciting Larkin's 'Church Going' in Arabic: 'A serious house on serious earth it is.'

PART FOUR

Europe

1

A little Norman tour

[May 1972]

I'm a hopeless holiday maker. I've tried it often enough, God knows: the brochures, advice from friends about the marvellous little place *they've* been to, the marvellous sounding little place I've always wanted to go to. But it never, in the event, really works. I can't get to grips with that prepared week or fortnight's break, can't come to any sort of easy terms with that empty space of time in foreign places. The business of actually getting there I don't mind at all. I like all the flummery, the careful nonsense of travel itself: the crisply milled traveller's cheques, like a packet of master forgeries in one's pocket, flourishing the past Odysseys of stamps and visas in my passport, the ridiculous embarkation and debarkation, customs and emigration forms, the pompous formality of the transport men in their glittering braid caps, the first whiffs of a foreign cigarette. All that cliché-ridden bustle and excitement of *physical* change goes down fine with me, sipping a Pernod in the boat deck saloon or watching a foreign spring come up from a train window vanishing southwards.

What worries me deeply is: *what am I going to do when I get there?* How, for example, am I going to fill the time between four and six o'clock tomorrow? I can always manage mornings abroad, with all that real fruit juice, crusty bread, *café au lait* and no papers. It's the afternoons that worry me. I'm sure you'll make at least two appropriate comments on these remarks: I'm being blasé and, in any case, it's not an original line. You've often felt exactly the same yourself about holidays, but have never dared say so in case *you* were thought blasé.

Well, let's admit the joint conspiracy and ask each other the same question: why is it that although, of course, we enjoy getting *away* from the normal run of home and work we still so often find it difficult to enjoy what we get *into*? The answer is pretty easy, surely. What do we usually get into?—rows with the management, hopelessly demeaning linguistic squabbles, sweating in charter flights (from fear as much as anything), bursting bladders in coaches, being dragged round incomprehensible museums and art galleries, sewage or a tanker full of oil all over the beaches; food poisoning, heat prostration—or just rain: all the suffering we accept, all that frenetic, punishing activity we have to give to filling those empty golden days . . . Why do we do it—spending millions on something which, in any objective light, can only be seen as pure hell?

I suppose the first and most obvious answer is that there is another and far more subtle conspiracy on the part of Messrs. Thos. Cook and his many descendants to make us believe that a holiday is, literally, the finest thing under the sun. 'Something for everyone' yell the brochures. 'Get away from it all'; 'A change is as good as a rest'. Wherever we turn there are these glittering, time-honoured quotes. And the assumption behind them is always perfectly clear: life is absolute hell—except when you take your holiday, (our address is on the back of the folder) when life becomes rip-roaring bloody fantastic. No effort is spared in hammering this message home since to let the idea arise for a moment that the quality and rewards of non-holiday life could be improved would be to endanger the rosy chocolate box foundations of an immense industry. Leisure is rapidly becoming more paying than work and we are going to be made to like it even if it kills us.

So let's go. They've cleaned the monuments over there, got their folksy dresses on and doubled the prices. We've had the brochures, a grim look from the bank manager and are now wracking our brains about what to do tomorrow and how we'll deal with that perennially insolent waiter. The whole business is an extraordinary trap to be caught in—so obvious, so painful. But of course the leisure merchants have realized that too, the essential masochism of the client which propels him into most holidays. All holidays are really a Dunkirk: we are so grateful, feel so lucky to return.

Well—quite coincidentally—the little place I've always had in my mind's eye was Honfleur, a hundred miles or so down the coast from Dunkirk, and its glittering green hinterland of Normandy. I'd never been anywhere in Normandy, so the whole area had a marvellous resonance for me. It appeared from books and films and picture postcards as a sort of super-England, an England of seventy years ago: full of two pre-war climates. There were proper farms there, like a child's game, with *every* sort of animal; lush fields, endless orchards and no new towns. There were genuine peasants with wooden pail-carriers round their necks; heavy earthenware bowls of pâté, chilled cider, Muscadet and lashings of sea food—all the succulent and various fish you can't get in England though we share exactly the same channel . . . cream, calvados and little country buses swaying over dusty lanes between real and massive hedges.

Normandy, I felt, just on my doorstep from Southampton, was the still living proof of many of the best things in life which we've so criminally dispensed with in England. Normandy was Jacque Tati's *Jour de Fête* in the country and Proust's *Jeunes Filles en Fleur* at the seaside. It had that essential ingredient of the best travel poster or brochure: it seemed, with absolute confidence, to suggest that there would be a mysterious fulfil-ment here: that in this place, and here alone, time would be re-gained, the lost years made good: a whole chunk of yourself would be returned to you, part self-knowledge, part innocence that had been buried in the dross of the world.

Of course, such travel views encourage one in the biggest lie as well—that there can be any sort of physical entry—or re-entry—into the magic garden: that getting away from, or moving towards *things* can get you into yourself. But when we set off for Honfleur this spring I thought nothing of this. I was the ideal client, suffering from a rough winter, hooked com-pletely on that room with a new view. The heavily embossed travellers cheques rubbed together in my pocket like fine sand-paper. The nice thing about them I suddenly realized, sipping a Pernod in the boat deck saloon, is that no one ever uses them more than once. They're always mint.

As it turned out the room in our Honfleur hotel had a splendid view, looking directly over the 'vieux basin' of the port, an Old Basin I was to become pretty familiar with in the coming days. . . .

Honfleur is the pretty little French fishing port to end all pretty little French fishing ports. One of the few towns in the province to completely escape damage in the last war, it sits on the mouth of the Seine, on the far side of the wide estuary from

Le Havre, like a mediaeval virgin, supremely satisfied with her refusals. And on the face of it the town has much to be satisfied about: above all by a coloured horseshoe of sixteenth- and seventeenth-century terraced buildings circling the Old Basin— the inner harbour—in wood and plaster, in blue and yellow and slate and a honey-coloured stone, looking over the bobbing fishing smacks and yachts, riding on one of the largest tide runs in the channel, twenty feet plus, so that before breakfast the gunwales were level with the quay and by lunchtime, when you were testing the first Muscadet on the terrace of *Au Gars Normand*, they were stuck in the mud like a routed navy far beneath you. The Old Basin itself maintained a constant level by means of a lock, crossed by a swing bridge, which was activated twice a day, according to the tides.

I could see at once, as we struggled with our luggage down from the bus stop to the hotel, that at least there was room for a lot of watching in Honfleur. The old and new basins, the whole sea front, was thick with watchers—watching the boats, the tourists, the tides, and above all waiting for the swing bridge to open. There were two wooden-fingered clocks on the Lieutenancy building advertising the next movement, and around these a small crowd lurked, covertly glancing up at the clocks and down at the water, waiting for the climax. There were those classic Frenchmen in blue overalls and berets, sucking yellow filter butts, and others—universal figures—in grubby macs carrying small suitcases; there were a lot of stage fishermen and a few genuine tourists—all rapt. Yes, I could see this was a promising pastime all right—and I began to plot my days. I reckoned I could fill every afternoon between four and six o'clock pretty easily now and I began to be quite charmed by the place.

But I should have remembered—there was the business of 'signing on' in the hotel to be got through: that great French debate about 'doubles' or 'singles', *salle avec bain* or *salle sans* everything; the half or the full pension, breakfast or no breakfast—a linguistic and financial obstacle course that would tax the resources of the French Academy and Paul Getty's accountants. And there was no doubt that we were in for the full works here. The Madame of the hotel was beautiful—but she was tough. We started off with no trouble. My verbs were working well. I was hitting the nouns first time round. We'd established a view over the 'vieux basin', double bed, bath, breakfast. And then I tried to beat her down to no 'pension' at all, and did she mind if we didn't have to eat in the hotel, only if we felt like it? Well, yes, she *would* mind, in fact. I started to root around for a few richly persuasive phrases. A well-heeled English couple came in the hall door behind us.

'Bonjour!' the Madame said, sliding effusively out to greet them from behind her stockade.

'Well, all right then,' I put in quickly. 'The demi-pension would be fine.'

We went upstairs, past a selection of splendid old French Line prints on the half-landing, those bitter-sweet transatlantic liners of the 'Thirties, the *France*, the *Columbie* and the *Paris*, the boats that Hemingway and Georges Carpentier and Marlene Dietrich used to spend alternate long week-ends on. I sat on the edge of our bed and counted my francs. First round to Madame, I thought. And then I wondered briefly if she'd ever miss one of those prints.

Then we got the guide book and the brochure out for the fifteenth time since we'd left Southampton: 'Honfleur, Calvados, 9120 habitants,' it said. 'Ville historique, un joyau pour les Artistes . . .' History, things to see, to do: 'Belles promenades aux environs de Honfleur, sports, equitation, pêche a la linge, jeu de boules, aero club, camping . . .' Everything—and there was plenty—was neatly catalogued. And it was then that I began to feel the first tinge of holiday despair creep over me: all these mysterious and unwanted 'activities' cropping up all round me, other people's plans and amusements being subtly forced on me: Who were these strange gentlemen so ready to play bowls with me on the Boulevard Charles V? And the staring boatman, beckoning to me from the Quai des Passagers?—and that haughty cavalry officer with the hunting crop on the chemin de Bruyères suggesting riding lessons and the other man, masked completely in a fur helmet and goggles with a Balkan cigarette in the corner of his mouth, offering me a 'cours de pilotage et promenades aeriennes' with him over Deauville? The brochure had suddenly become dangerously peopled. I saw the local *syndicat d'initiative* now as a subversive organization intent on raising all the holiday ghosts of my past—all the things I should have done, and never had, on trips long ago: bowls, riding, fishing

and even flying a small bi-plane over the dunes against the
sea wind. I could actually see the wooden struts, the canvas
fuselage, the old-fashioned barometric gauges in the open cockpit, and the little curved wind shield with its brass adjusters on
either side. I was being threatened with pleasure. I felt exposed,
watched, followed, pursued by an impossible glut of excitements.

And there is an uncomfortable corollary to this sense of holiday exposure: being made to feel on the run makes one begin to
look for shelter; one wants to avoid the public events and places
and to eavesdrop on the endless cameos of ordinary life about
you. A walk down a foreign village street at midday can give
one the strongest sense of exile: those figures glimpsed through
a flapping curtain or doorway, bent over a stove or radio. The
smell of strange gravies, the vital, yet incomprehensible chatter
from the capital, the clatter and hum of someone else's lunchtime. The heavy tasselled sideboard in the front parlour with the
dark framed photographed dead, archaic faces from a world, or a
civil war; or the happy, silver-bordered image of a girl before first
communion. A woman turning a mattress, Grandfather shaving
from a pail of water, a boy doing his homework. These domestic
interiors, proffered intimacies—sudden, intense, transient—are
like lifelines thrown at one all down the street, perfect sanctuaries
that one can never penetrate. I let the Honfleur guide fall to the
floor, sick with its pressing invitations, and we slept till evening.

There are, of course, marvellous moments in being away from
it all. And I shouldn't give the impression that I think a holiday
is, by definition, something quite without glamour. It's just that
the glamour has nothing to do with our, or the local tourist
board's expectations. The good things in being abroad are small,
uncalled-for moments, essences—a heightened state of awareness
which one can honestly say is due to the fresh surroundings, the
oblique angles one has to take in looking at things away from
home. We *are* strangers and there are times when this pays
curious and imaginative dividends.

We'd walked right round the horseshoe before supper and
had taken seats at a café on the far side of the Old Basin, next to
the town hall. To our left was a building with a ladies' hairdressers on the ground floor and a dentist's plaque—with his
rooms above presumably. I'd thrown my English cigarettes
away, now properly into the burnt French brands, and we were

just considering a second apéritif when a woman came out of the doorway, tidy, in a headscarf and sensible shoes. She was one of those classic French women, thirtyish, assured yet pliant, hard but with distinct intimations of abandon. One has seen something of her sort in French films from Arletty in *Les Enfants du Paradis* onwards: through early Michele Morgan, *Quai des Brumes*, Martine Carol, *Le Diable au Corps* to Jeanne Moreau in *Les Amants*. Yet for all her fictional provenance, her cinema verite, she remains quite mysterious. A Madame Bovary or the wife of the baker? Even Maigret, I thought, couldn't have placed her, the quiet, provocative woman walking down the quay that spring evening. And that was when the moment, the epiphany, came to me. Who was she? Had she been to the dentist or to the hairdressers? And if the former, was she perhaps his mistress, for it was late in the day for teeth? And if with the hairdresser was it in preparation for a night out with her husband—or with her lover? Perhaps her husband was away, or at sea . . . ? The permutations were endless. But I preferred my first theory: the dentist was her lover and all her husband knew was that she suffered badly from her gums and had them massaged every Tuesday. And then I was away, the imagination soared. Just think of it, an affair amidst all that metal paraphernalia—the instruments of pain, the probes, the drills and hypodermics. I supposed he would start by leaning over her, the mechanics of the huge chair sighing gently as he tipped it into the horizontal . . .

What nonsense, you may say. No French dentist would risk being struck off the register, least of all in a town of only 9120 'habitants'. But then, I thought, no *affaire* worth the name is without risk, and the French have a tradition in these matters. I was prepared to confirm my suspicions. And from then on I was able to experience freely all the romance of France without any of the discomfort, rudeness or expense that normally attend that experience. The lady and the dentist could have my holiday for me, for I supposed that every now and then they would contrive to get away from Honfleur, the husband out at sea again no doubt: a silver Citroën on the road to Paris, lilacs in the Luxembourg or chestnuts in the Bois de Boulogne—for it had gone through the seasons, this *affaire*. It was lasting, it was true: the little unnoticed commercial hotel on the wrong side of the

Étoile, meals at a restaurant behind St. Lazare which only they knew, had only known together. One could even go as far as thinking that the dentist had a permanent room out by the Porte des Lilas, that there had been accordions there on Saturday nights, a Bal Musette, and a man like Brassens in a café afterwards with a guitar. Once, maybe, they'd even managed a long week-end travelling easily in September down the Loire, living in the world, drinking the wine . . . Now that the sort of thing I do like about holidays—the opportunities it gives for exercising the imagination, which a view of a woman from a saloon bar in Earl's Court might not do.

We went back to the hotel for supper. And the lady?—to her husband no doubt. 'How are your gums?' I could hear him asking her kindly at that very moment. 'Better?'

For the rest of the week we watched and we slept and we did the sights—attacked with diminishing enthusiasm the mounds of *moules* served everywhere in small restaurants of repute about the port and came to know the ecology and stonework of the Old Basin better than any ninety-year-old 'habitant'. We really put our backs into it.

But as the days passed I noticed another holiday infection gradually taking hold of me. Instead of improving, my grasp of the language began to fade. From those first fine flights with Madame it had become a completely untrustworthy thing, a menacing sort of semaphore. I became like a defective child with one or two utterly trivial and inexact phrases which I used again and again, whatever the context. At such times, with a waiter or with Madame, provoked beyond endurance, I would break into a terrible pent-up pidgin English, waving my hands in the air, like a prophet defying the apocalypse. In the afternoons I began to haunt the news-stands in search of a Continental *Daily Mail*, a sure sign that the end is near. The infection came to a head one night when, on returning late from a meal, we found the front door of the hotel locked; we'd forgotten to ask for an outside key. When Madame at last appeared it was in a long nightdress and a genuine red nightcap, the sort with a tail and bobble on it. I've said she was tough. Now she was fierce as well, like the wolf suddenly unmasked in Little Red Riding Hood. She gobbled us up in a thrash of the most extremely irate French that I was powerless to combat.

'Mais oui,' I started. 'Mais . . .' But nothing more emerged. It was as if the sound had suddenly been turned off. Far from either arguing or apologizing with her I was unable to remember the simplest words—for 'door' or 'key' or 'sorry' or 'how dare you!' Nothing. Her language flowed over me like a glacier. I seized up completely.

So there it was. Communication was at an end. And there seemed little point in doing dumb battle throughout the rest of Normandy. Better to go back and remember Henry V, thankful to be abed in England. We left for Le Havre next morning. Honfleur had become *Marienbad* in that private film show of mine. And I realized now the significance of all the mysterious strangers that had taken horrible life for me in the Honfleur guide. They were the cast: the rotund, silent little men in caps offering a game of bowls; the staring, beckoning boatmen on the evening tide; the officer flicking his jodphurs viciously with a riding crop and the pilot running a Balkan cigarette around his lips . . . They were rising up again now, gathering in the shadows of the bedroom. A collective indictment. It was time to run, for tomorrow they would be unavoidable, implacable.

Perhaps I need a holiday?—and a firmly packaged one at that.

2

Time of the thousand francs

Now and again, years afterwards, polite hostesses, immigration officials and deaf aunts I've not seen in years—ask me what I do. 'I work in films' used to be my ultimate and very guarded reply. Usually I manage to dodge the issue altogether—offering instead either a lie, or else a wise smile as evidence of some very confidential pursuit. The truth is that quite a few outsiders still look on the film industry with suspicion—as a retreat for hysterics, idlers and ne'er-do-wells; a vulgar dream factory, a world in which money is at once no object and the only object—an emporium of glitter and deceit where the camera lies with every click of the shutter.

Yet there's often, I feel, a degree of envy in this sort of distaste—a small thought at the back of their disapproval which suggests that, well, perhaps after all it might be nice, once in a while—just to see what it was like—to drink champagne with Otto and Sam, with Marlene and Liz, while speeding together through the night in a chartered express en route to some exotic location, to be drowned in a chorus of imperious orders given by men with guttural accents, black eye patches and astrakhan collars . . .

But of course, 'all this' is a dream. The industry isn't like that anymore and hasn't been for years. Very little of it these days is either 'outrageous' or 'extravagant'. Films today are made by accountants and not by imperious moguls. Their heyday—and that of a whole era of unabashed vulgarity and excess—has gone. However, in one of my last moments with the movies a few years ago, I did experience a little of what it must all have been like.

Eddy, as I shall have to call him, an American producer I'd heard of but never met, wrote asking me if I'd work on a film treatment of a novel by a prominent Frenchman. We corresponded—or rather his secretary and I exchanged a few brief notes. Eddy, she said, was coming to Europe the following month and would I come with him and his 'assistant' to Paris to discuss the project with the French eminence? Certainly I would. And who wouldn't. It was a cold, nasty spring in England that year and I've never turned down trips to Paris.

Our rendezvous struck an unusual note from the word go. I'd been told on the 'phone to wait for Eddy at the barrier leading to The Golden Arrow platform at Victoria. That was all. I wasn't to look for anyone, just wait. I waited. A moment before the train was due to leave there was a flurry of porters, a sound of honking and the station loudspeakers suddenly and inexplicably changed brake into the 'Post Horn Gallop'. I turned and there was Eddy. I was quite sure. There was no doubt. He was strutting behind a mountain of luggage followed meekly by his 'assistant'. It was Caesar setting out on a campaign and the introductions were suitably curt—a nasal, mid-Atlantic 'Good to have you with us' which seemed to suggest my function as a mere dragoman to the party—and we were bustling down the platform, splitting up tender goodbyes, barging through innumerable last messages—as if the station, the train, the platform—indeed the whole concept of transportation—had been something created for our convenience alone.

Eddy, a mountainous six-footer, sported an ankle-length camel-hair coat set off by dancing pumps and a pearly tie; on one finger an emerald immersed in solid gold; on top a very splendid and carefully tended expanse of white hair; sixtyish, very jowled, with sad, benign eyes. His 'assistant' on the other hand was completely, inflexibly English, the epitome of middle-class respectability and discretion—clerical-grey topcoat, Anthony Eden hat, tie from a good regiment, a wan, fortyish face—everything was right except that when he spoke, which wasn't often, it was in broad Cockney. His only baggage appeared to be a costly looking black leather briefcase, cornered and clasped in real brass.

We were ushered into what seemed like a whole half-carriage of the train, walled off from the rest. In the middle—a round table covered by a crisp white cloth, a bowl of tulips and the morning papers—*all* the morning papers. At Clapham junction we were offered a choice of caviare, chicken or smoked salmon sandwiches. Some few minutes afterwards, while passing through a more than usually ugly example of Victorian urban development—and without our being offered *any* choice—a bottle of champagne was presented on a rickety stand. At Dover, due to immediate and substantial largesse on the part of the 'assistant' we were shot through customs, put on board before anyone else and installed in what might have been the Captain's private quarters. However, the boat had hardly got under way before Eddy decided that the first-class lounge might be a better 'situation'. Chairs were gathered round a table within nodding distance of the bar and a bottle of brandy arrived. The 'assistant' didn't have any. Instead he looked anxiously at Eddy as he poured himself a large one, which he topped up with Malvern water. There was a pause. I thought this was the moment when Eddy would signal a start to our discussion about the 'project'. But not at all. He embarked on quite a different scenario—his own life story. Of how he had been born in England and come out to the States in the early 'Twenties, had been a cattle hand, had then just 'found' himself in Hollywood and had at once been offered work as an extra riding horses in Westerns. This phase of his life, in which he respectfully described himself as an 'artist', had only occupied him a moment or two. At once he had formed his own company and become a producer. From the mid-'Twenties onwards he had been responsible for a vast number of films—most of them potboilers but some which had become famous examples of the cinema in that ebullient period. It was a fascinating description. Then suddenly, half-way through a more than usually glittering episode, he stopped, looked suspiciously around him and summoned a waiter. 'These fellows around here, up there at the bar, they're not first class— what's the idea? I and my friends—we *paid* to be here.' The threat was ominous. The waiter loped off, returned in a moment with a bevy of Pursers and in a few minutes the lounge had been virtually cleared. Eddy had been right. Only a fraction of the people had been *real* first-class passengers. 'I have this sixth sense about who *fits* in a place,' Eddy growled while the 'assistant' and I swapped a nervous glance. In the sudden hush Eddy continued with his story—the barman and the few genuine plutocrats left followed it cautiously but intently.

Before we docked at Calais Eddy, the 'assistant' and the smart leather bag withdrew to the cabin, and Eddy emerged later looking much perkier. The 'assistant's' function, though still not exactly clear, appeared to be of a medical nature.

The dimensions of our compartment on the journey to Paris were the same as they'd been on the English side. Only this time our private quarters were laid out as a dining-room. Everything was impeccably nostalgic and elaborately Edwardian, like a Rex Whistler drawing. Cut glass twinkled beneath small silver lamps at each place. There was pale wood panelling and four blue-eyed plaster cherubs at each corner supported the moulded ceiling. The window was particularly unexpected. It was very long and stuck out beyond the sides of the other carriages so that one had an uninterrupted view up or down the line just by leaning one's head a little to one side. Underneath it was a complicated legend in several languages—'It is inadvisable to throw weighty objects from this window while the train is in motion since their velocity increases in proportion to the speed at which the vehicle is travelling.' There followed a table of ratios. I could see no communication cord. I suppose it was assumed that in such well-appointed, opulent surroundings the disappearance of even one's nearest and dearest should not give rise to the slightest alarm.

The lunch, which was 'presented with the compliments of Maxim's, Paris', was of endless variety and splendour. It went through seven courses and lasted—due to Eddy's habit of ordering some courses twice over—all of the four hours which it took to reach our destination. Both the 'assistant' and I held our tongues throughout most of the meal while Eddy, with increasing exaggeration and relish, continued with his life history. 'So what do you think this Jean Harlow said to me . . . ? Yes, Harold Lloyd—when I first met Harold Lloyd . . .' And of an actress who'd never made it—'She had a great talent and a lively mind, a beautiful person—if it hadn't been for that affair with a greyhound in the back of a taxi . . .' One bizarre episode followed another. One after another these celluloid ghosts were sprung, blazed a moment into life through Eddy's words and gestures, then died again. Outside the pale yellows and greens of the Normandy spring slipped by, the afternoon gradually subsided and then it was dark.

When we got to Paris we were ferried to the hotel in a sort of private ambulance in which Eddy lay down and we two perched at his elbow like undertakers transporting an emperor to his tomb. Eddy mumbled some concluding details of his history, bringing his life, in a few half-hearted phrases, to what for him was clearly an inadequate and unsatisfying present. Paris melted by behind the dark glass of the car. It was the sort of glass you can only see *out* of, so that *we* could see all the glitter of Paris, but Paris and its people could see nothing of us. We slipped into the city like actors into the wings, taking their cue. It was appropriate. The image of dark glass has been a perennial one in the Cinema: From Eddy, through Garbo to Monroe—to see but not be seen, perhaps because in reality, such people have nothing to hide.

And then, as we moved through the huge pillars that form the entrance to the Crillon Hotel and on into the sparkle of the foyer beyond—amidst this culmination of lavish circumstance which would have formed an adequate setting for one of his early epics—Eddy cheered up once more.

'Home again,' he sighed and went off to look over some silk ties on display by the lift. 'My lift?' he asked the attendant innocently when it arrived. The 'assistant' quickly slipped the boy a 1000 francs, the doors snapped shut on some other hapless guests, and we sped upwards. That was in the time of 1000 franc notes, when people like Eddy lived the films they couldn't make, when there was no penny-pinching and films weren't an art.

3

Tunbridge Wells

[December 1971]

George Orwell wrote somewhere about coming back through south-east England from the political horrors of Europe: through a complacent, reassuring, gentle land of sleek cows, suet puddings and red pillar-boxes, an England from which only bombs would wake us. When you get to Tunbridge Wells—through just that same sort of land—you have just the same sort of feeling. Though the bombs have come and gone, one would know nothing of all that here: of Alma, Sedan and Inkerman—yes, one would learn of these things certainly, distant skirmishes with the infidel. But that policemen had worn guns for many years, that genocide and the midnight knock on the door were old hat a hundred miles or so across the Channel, such ideas would be like oaths in the many chapels and churches of Tunbridge Wells.

The facts of life never seem to have impinged very much on this town. Founded on the sparkling fantasies of its water cure in 1606 and continuing its fine flights under Beau Nash in the eighteenth century, it reached its apotheosis under Queen Victoria as the richest and most exclusive retiring-rooms in the Empire. It's always 1884 in Tunbridge Wells, never 1984. Yet because of its undisturbed and isolated Englishness it represents very well today Orwell's divided and complex patriotism: here, in aspic, is all the Imperial pretence and paraphernalia that he loathed, all the architectural and emotional heritage of the old and silly, the snobby and privileged. But here too, equally preserved in the grand houses on the hills and in the wretched little commercial streets by the goods station, are many of the things Orwell liked about England: 'bathrooms, armchairs, brown bread, marmalade and beer made with veritable hops' in the grand houses, and that intense, impoverished privateness of English life in the mean streets: huge blooms in every back patch, football pools being checked off beside endless radios all along

135

the street, the sense everywhere of passionate hobbies going on in the coal shed or front parlour—pigeon-fancying or stamp-collecting or wireless telegraphy—and an addiction to those little stationers' shops that one still sees in Tunbridge Wells with their libraries of do-it-yourself magazines, the staider comics, liquorice, Woodbines and rude postcards. Orwell probably would have loathed Tunbridge Wells, yet it retains very much the emotional colouring of his world and that of others of his pre-war class and generation. Here are the absolute opposite poles of 'England, his England', and I think he would have been surprised to see these essences of English wealth and poverty surviving so vigorously thirty years after the various dooms he forecast for them.

But Tunbridge Wells has always been a place of extremes and excesses, of rich and poor, ever since the third Lord North discovered the original spring while riding back from a three months' stay with Lord Bergavenny in 1606. Lord North had gone to ground with his friend for another sort of 'cure'—one made necessary by forty days' non-stop drinking with King Christian of Denmark at the court of James I. The Stuarts weren't used to an intake of such quantity and potency and there were many very sore heads indeed in England that summer. Lord North himself felt at death's door, and his three months on the wagon in the country seem to have made him worse. But then, the apparent miracle: the steely-tasting, ochre-coloured waters bubbling up in the sunlight of the little grove in the forest made him feel better at once and he took as many bottles as he could with him back to London. A physician there confirmed that the water contained iron and a substance known as 'vitriol': an ingredient, in those days, considered of great medicinal value, curing colic, melancholy and the vapours, killing flatworm in the belly and loosening the clammy humours of the body.

Lord North's hangover began to improve, and by the following spring, as soon as the tracks were passable, he was back post-haste for a prolonged cure at the wells—Tunbridge Wells as it became known from the town of Tonbridge five miles away, and eventually Royal Tunbridge Wells, by proclamation of Edward VII in 1909. The first of the Royals was Henrietta Maria, the French wife of Charles I, who came and camped on the common next to the wells in 1629, and from then on it was Royals most of the way, culminating with Queen Victoria who spent her summers here as a princess but who came only once after her accession, with Prince Albert in 1849. But by then royal patronage hardly mattered. Tunbridge Wells had long before established itself as the first and most popular of the specifically 'English' watering-places. Bath and Buxton, the only two spas which preceded it, were, of course, Roman baths and not nearly so convenient to the court in London.

In the seventeenth century, after the Restoration, Tunbridge Wells began properly to bloom, and perhaps one of the more curious and most noticeable aspects of the town dates from just before this period. Two of the main thoroughfares are called Mount Ephraim and Mount Sion, and the place is littered with other Old Testament solemnities, Revivalist place-names and Presbyterian memories. Yet the area was strongly Royalist. It seems that some of Cromwell's Ironsides were encamped on hills above the town and it was they who first gave the wells its strong and lasting Nonconformist flavour. These Dissenters became the local inhabitants and tradespeople, strongly disapproving of the summer visitors who later came to infest the place, though willing enough to take their money off them for lodgings and suchlike.

But meanwhile, more important than the ministers, were the water doctors, as always in the eighteenth- and nineteenth-century spa business furiously bent on persuading everyone that water was thicker than blood. A certain Dr. Madan of the Wells in 1687 went further than most, at least in his language. 'The Tunbridge waters,' he wrote, 'are impregnated with a calcanthous or vitriolate juice; which, with its sulphurous particles, irritates and moves the belly to a blackish excretion and by frequent drinking thereof blackeneth the tongue, because this member, being of a spongy substance, imbibes some sooty sulphurous minims into its porosity, occasioning this tincture.' That the waters induced fecundity was another number-one selling point as far as the doctors were concerned. One of them speaks of how their 'spirituous ferment naturally incites men and women to amorous emotions and titillations, being previous dispositions enabling them to procreation'. With water like that how could you go wrong? And the good doctors didn't.

The elegant yet rather silly and sad Beau Nash, fresh from his triumphs as Master of Ceremonies at Bath, came next to Tunbridge Wells, taking over the same polite function there in 1735, and for the rest of the century the place was at its greatest height. And this is the period when we probably know it best, when the tree-lined walks by the Wells were properly laid out and became the Pantiles of today; when assembly- and gaming-rooms, coffee shops and the fine 170-yard-long colonnade, went up on either side of the walk and fashionable society, practically *en masse*, took their summer sport there, the waters being hardly more than an excuse for wandering up and down, for chattering and flirting, gambling and whoring, with that elegantly contrived eighteenth-century abandon that died to the rattle of a spinning-jenny. It was the foppish, gossipy, scandalous but highly literate and witty world of Dr. Johnson, Garrick, Colley Cibber, and the novelist Samuel Richardson, who came to the Wells to discuss the intimate affairs of a certain young lady called Clarissa with Colley and with Dr. Young, of *Night Thoughts* fame, who was particularly anxious that the young lady in question should suffer the greatest distress and misery possible. Several years later the woes of *Clarissa* became the rage of England, so that if the airs of Tunbridge Wells nurtured only one English novelist it was at least the first.

But the sparky flummery didn't last: it never does. The Nonconformists and the conforming middle classes won the day, and by the coming of Queen Victoria and the railways Tunbridge Wells had settled into very strict, if equally comfortable ways. And this is the town that one sees today: three or four towns really, spread about the Biblical hills with great open parks and woods and fields in between—quite like Addis Ababa in this respect, if in absolutely no other. And like so many of these disbanded spa towns in England, having lost the *raison d'être* of its waters yet become richer still on the pensions of the Empire, it has not searched for any other role, so that great hunks of the nineteenth century are preserved intact. There is talk of the industrial estate on the outskirts, of 'arterial roads and bypasses', as motorways are called here, of drugs and maxi-skirts, but the tones are those of the proud old aristocrats in Auden's poem:

> The Outer Provinces are lost,
> Unshaven horsemen swill

The great wines of the Châteaux
Where you danced long ago.

Tunbridge Wells remains indomitably Victorian, with all the
strict gradations of architecture and class which that era required: the houses rising up the hills, from the back-to-backs in
Commercial Road, up through the shopkeepers' decorated semis
of Beulah Road, to the magnificent crescent of Italianate villas in
the twenty-six acres of Calverley Park, designed by Decimus
Burton in 1828 and to my mind the finest urban estate and
landscaping in Britain. Beyond this are the Edwardian suburbs
of the town, Roedean Road and sombre Warwick Park, and here
the empty pavements slope up and down endlessly, as wide as
roads in other towns, on roads as wide as boulevards, bounding
the colossal whims and follies of the time, red-brick palaces
behind twenty- and even thirty-foot embankments of evergreens
and an assortment of never-picked fruit trees and bushes. When
I was there this autumn, on a day of stagnant purple clouds and
slowly drifting bonfires, my feet squelched over a carpet of huge
blackberries while brilliant red apples bounced off the road here
and there in the long distances in front of me. I must have
walked for at least two miles about these gloomy palatial drives
and saw only one other person, apart from a huge old lady in
black, a giantess from a nightmare, whose face shone out at me
unwaveringly from the depths of a bow-window, fiddling with
her pearls.

Later that afternoon, when a chill had come up with a misty
rain, I heard those unforgettable and infinitely threatening voices
of childhood raised behind a double holly hedge: a prep school,
with the louts of Shell A getting in a quick bit of bullying
behind the bicycle shed before Sunday tea—bread and remnants-
of-Empire butter, muffins and plum jam on the staff table. One
was back with Orwell again, *Such, such were the joys*, and I
remembered the second-hand school outfitters I'd noticed near
my hotel: the second-hand school trunks in the window, sinister
iron maidens, graveyards for so many Willoughbys and Smiths;
the lacrosse and hockey sticks, discarded running spikes, the
other implements of pain. The braid had tarnished on the caps
and blazers; moth and beetle and damp lay in wait for the rest of
these littered remains of the white man's burden. But they were

not quite done yet. 'As good as new for half the price,' it had
said in the window. And I thought: 'England, your England' is
still alive and struggling in Tunbridge Wells.

4

Malvern

[December 1971]

It was my first visit to Malvern and yet I knew I'd been there
before: the railway sloping up the valley to the neat little Gothic
station; the grotesquely ornamented granite Victorian mansions
—from a distance like a row of gargoyles on shelves, one above
the other, going up the hills—and then the evergreens, the
almost exotic flowers and shrubs and trees of high places;
the faint rumour of an expensive deodorant. And finally, on the
early September week I was there, an intense blue sky and a
heat that was somehow sharp with intimations of frost—sweat
around the shoulder-blades but one's ankles shivered. This had
all happened to me somewhere else: this quintessential Englishness, this rich flowering of Victorian Gothic, this arrogance,
lunacy and structural daring, this Jerusalem on a hill-top. I
looked up at the skyline from the porch of my hotel: a steeple,
pine trees and a bird wheeling slowly round in the warm rising
currents. And then I remembered all at once: the bird had been
an eagle above the station in Simla, the hills had been the Himalayas, the steeple the parish church at the end of the Mall there,
the spiky mansions had been the suburbs of that Imperial hill
station and the intense, glittering sky had been the sky of India
three years ago. There were merely geographical differences:
Simla was 5,000 miles away and 6,000 feet higher up; Simla
was in the State of Himachal Pradesh and Malvern in Worcester-
shire. But in creation and mood, almost in lay-out, they were
identical: two Victorian hill stations where the industrial or
administrative Raj came to get away from it all: for pleasures
sadly or for the Viceroy's pecking-order parties, for the water
cure or to build granite institutions for their offspring. The ambitions behind the two towns were the same—godliness, health,
education, above all duty, duty in all things—and nothing could
better illustrate the lordly universality of the Victorian mind
than a trip to these two places on successive week-ends.

These nineteenth-century spas and hill stations were really
upper-class Butlin holiday camps where the *nouveau riche* from
the Black Country and the well-bred from the Home Counties
could punish themselves for their mental and physical excesses
on the plains—take themselves down a peg or two, almost in
sight of God and out of sight of the menials. They were pre-
serves for a species now almost extinct, the high-minded men.
Only the architecture now remains in both towns: the wonder-
fully excessive decoration, the mixture of Scottish Baronial,
mock-Jacobean and pseudo-Italianate buildings, the steep tiling,
the flowery castellation, mock battlements, fairy-tale towers,
mad steeples and oriel windows—buildings as strange as the
Pyramids, homes for men who had been gods and who are as
distant now as the Pharaohs.

I thought of these people on my first afternoon in Malvern,
walking the long, tree-littered lower roads of the town: Graham
Road, Albert Road, Clarence Road, Victoria Road, the huge
houses in their acre plots, each insultingly different from its
neighbours, lurking behind a forest of laurel and rhododendron
—for the first and continuously overwhelming impression one
has of the town is of the extraordinary vigour and quirky
imagination of its creators. Malvern must be one of the most
perfect reflections anywhere of that mid-Victorian explosion into
'good works', when there was money to spare from the mines
and steel mills for crafts and design, for eccentricities and
excrescences generally: fluted pillar-boxes, pagoda porches and
stained-glass windows in the drawing-room. And that is what
one immediately wants to know in Malvern: who *were* these
people, whose presence lies so thick about the place that modern
Malvern, by comparison, seems the creation of a pygmy race in
stature and ambition?

Of course it was the waters that first brought them here:
taking the waters, the water cure; cleanliness next to godliness;
you drank it, bathed in it, lived with it up to your ears, inside
and out. In 1800 Malvern was a small thatched village of 800
people with a coaching inn on a rackety road through the hills.
Fifty years later, even before the railway came, it had become a
town of more than five thousand, with almost as many visitors
in a year. What drove the Victorians to the waters? Was it a
spiritual more than a physical cleansing they were after—since

even then the medical efficacy of the cure was widely doubted?
A search for an English Jordan in Malvern, Buxton, Tunbridge
Wells and Leamington? For it is surely no coincidence that
many of the spas developed next door to the industrial horrors
and slag-heaps of the North and the Midlands: a washing of
guilty hands under that rich Victorian canopy of self-improve-
ment? For whatever reasons, the moment called forth the men.
In Malvern it was Doctors Wilson and Gully who opened the
sluice gates, basing their cures and equipment on those of the
pioneer waterman, Vincent Priessnitz from Graefenburg in
Silesia, with whom Wilson had studied the previous year. The
Malvern hills seemed the nearest and nicest equivalent to the
Alpine circumstances of the German spa, and the good doctors
imported a German band and a quantity of alpenstocks just to
be sure of setting the right mood. They were in business. And
what a business it was.

Brian Smith's history of Malvern is the best guide to the town.
The clients—and they soon included such otherwise hard-
headed notables as Macaulay and Florence Nightingale, as well
as Dickens, Gladstone, Wordsworth and Darwin—were roused at
five o'clock, stripped, and immediately wrapped in dripping
damp sheets, then covered tightly in blankets. After an hour or
so of this, buckets of water were thrown at them. Then they
were pushed out onto the hills, each with his 'Graefenburg
flask' and alpenstock, where they had to drink their way round
all the wells—a five-mile trot with the waters lurching with ever
increasing momentum about the bowels. A breakfast of dry
biscuits and more water was followed by the really serious baths
—sitz baths, shallow baths, running sitz baths, hip baths, the
Neptune Girdle (a cold compress round the stomach removed
only for meals), and an extraordinarily dangerous affair known
as the lamp bath in which the client, wrapped in his damp sheets
again, sat in a patent chair with a burning lamp under his back-
side. Finally, if the cure was going well, you had the cold douche:
a hogshead of iced water dropped on you from twenty feet
through a three-inch pipe. 'Dinner invariably consisted of boiled
mutton and fish' and 'bed followed early,' the history relates.
One is surprised that the tomb didn't follow even sooner.

The punishment prices started at five guineas a week; servants'
quarters were extra and you supplied your own blankets and

sheets. No wonder Dr. Gully was soon making more than £10,000 a year out of it all. Yet, of course, it wasn't simply a fake: there were many 'cures'. For the bloated, overworked, indulgent Victorian paterfamilias a month on such a regimen could hardly but improve his sagging constitution. And that was the real secret of the 'cure', though few of the doctors admitted it. It was galloping round those hills plus the fish and boiled mutton, far more than the waters, that did the trick. Malvern boomed as the water flowed, until the last decades of the century when the whole thing quietly faded out. Doctors Gully and Wilson had gone—their extremely forceful personalities had much to do with the success of the cure—and people travelled more readily abroad now, preferring the far easier Continental water cure, which included casinos and Strasbourg paté. Today, only St. Ann's Well, immediately above the town, remains: a charming octagonal tower on the steep side of the hill where cokes and crisps and postcards are more popular than the stuttering marble-scalloped fountain in an annexe next door.

After a frugal breakfast next morning I struggled up to the well myself and had a few copious draughts. It was nice enough but seemed soft and tasteless as rainwater. And I remembered that was another problem the watery doctors had: how to persuade their masochistic clients that something which didn't taste extremely nasty could be any good for you. They got round this mainly by telling the truth: Malvern water is famed not for what it contains but for what it doesn't—it lacks almost all impurities while still retaining the necessary mineral and other salubrious qualities.

Then there were the hills and I was off round them—severely under-watered by Victorian standards, and all the better for it. The hill paths are public and I wondered how Gladstone and Florence Nightingale had managed those other calls of nature on their whistle-stop tour of the wells. I supposed there had been glorious Gothic conveniences, magnificently-tiled urinals, dotted here and there in the bushes, disguised as follies or game lodges—Darwin pondering the species and Wordsworth the lack of daffodils from a mock-Norman arrow-slit overlooking the valley.

Certainly the views and the hills themselves are impressive. And there is something mildly Alpine about them, odd aspects which are wild and strange: the dipping, swerving, steeply rising paths, great pre-Cambrian boulders, a sudden chasm with a sheer drop hundreds of feet into a black volcanic or quarry lake, a huge shoulder of gorse and fern and beyond it another drop—a thousand feet—into Herefordshire: the whole thing a sort of miniaturized Alps. With the spiky, turreted Victorian town far beneath and the midday train from Paddington crawling up the valley, it's the sort of setting where one wouldn't be at all surprised to see Holmes and Watson striding over the brow of a hill. Nor would Professor Moriarty seem out of place, sneering behind a loose boulder on the path to the quarry.

Malvern, of course, is much more Shaw and Elgar than Conan Doyle. Shaw came here every year, right through the 'Thirties, when Sir Barry Jackson's company presented his plays at the Festival Theatre, and Elgar spent much of his formative time here before and after 1900. The two men became close friends, in fact, verbally back-slapping each other in a chummy, clubby way. Shaw particularly was a great hero at Malvern, planting commemorative trees in the Winter Gardens, doing the rounds of the Festival garden parties in his Jaeger outfit and generally playing the lad. What, one wonders, did this essential Irishman see in this essence of England? The Bravos of the great middle class perhaps—acceptance by that class which had ostracized his family in early youth and whom he had later pilloried in his work, for Shaw's childhood in Dublin had been penny-pinching Victorian genteel, with rumours of illegitimacy. Now, in Malvern, he could show how he had pulled himself up and out of it all by his bootstraps, and could dine with Elgar and the Town Council to the strains of 'Land of Hope and Glory'.

Malvern was the creation of a burgeoning nineteenth-century middle class, who by the turn of the century and after, were anxious to spread their cultural wings a bit: Shaw and Elgar perfectly reflected their cultural ambitions. And today, though the Festival is gone, Malvern's visitors are still mainly the new rich or the old poor from the industrial Midlands. A hundred years ago they flocked to the spa by train on day-trips from Wolverhampton, much to the annoyance of Lady Foley who owned most of the property in the town, and now the same sort of people, from the same sort of places, come in cheap two-seaters or packed coaches, just for the overnight stop. Now, as then, the local inhabitants have little to do with them; the real money comes from the winter conferences, the twenty-odd boarding schools and the Royal Radar Establishment headquarters there, its huge scanning dish ominously patrolling the hills and the valley. The blustering colonels and withered ladies are still to be seen about town, but it's really not their season any more in Malvern.

What does remain—and remains Malvern's most fascinating element—is their grandparents' houses, as well as the satellite shops and hotels. These buildings were first of all meant to last, yet having indubitably allowed for this, the designers let themselves go in ornament. Together, these two qualities of durability and decor make Malvern a perfect three-dimensional Victorian scrapbook. There is much pomposity, but unlike other nineteenth-century remnants, it has humour as well. Dr. Gully, for example, built himself two extraordinary houses for his water cure—still there today as the Tudor Hotel. One was excessively Scottish Baronial, the other severe mock-Jacobean—one for the men, the other for the ladies. Then, with sudden mad inspiration, he connected the two together by means of a splendid Venetian bridge: the Bridge of Sighs. But perhaps 'The Priory', built in 1874 and now the seat of the Town Council, is the most sensational building left in Malvern. Its interior design, with elaborately-carved pinewood ceilings and marble fireplaces as big as tunnel openings, includes a series of remarkable domestic stained-glass windows. The overall motif is the natural world of Aesop's Fables: flowers, grasses, trees and above all animals. The draughtsmanship suggests the world of Beatrix Potter thirty years before she started on her stories: the colouring and mood are almost exactly hers. On the main staircase, rising up two floors, is a cathedral-like window—in mock-Perpendicular, of course. A huge frog on a water-lily, a real Jeremy Fisher, is offering a fox a bottle of medicine marked 'Please shake me.' The fox, a glorious animal in deep yellows and browns and golds, is winking. And there is much more of the same delicate anthropomorphism: a stork turns away in bad-tempered disgust; mottled carp and perch swim doubtfully in the dreamy green waters beneath; a blue frieze of chattering birds and squirrels warns from above. Who had commissioned this inspired hodgepodge, where the separate architectural moods of 500 years have been gathered together and baked into a cake of rich fantasy? And who had commanded the glass—that permanent magic-lantern show for the children as they played along the landings through the wet afternoons? We have an image of the Victorians as repressed, puritanical, often unimaginative people. Yet Malvern proves differently, spotlighting their other faces, their vigorous fancies, their strange and witty conceits.

5

Infinite Possibilities

[June 1974]

Most of us cherish a very personal notion about those parts of south-eastern Europe which used to be called the Balkans—strong visions and preconceptions about the area, both in historical fact and through fiction. What do we see, for example, if we shuffle quickly through our minds picking out all the cards in the fiction file marked 'Balkans'? First of all the whole pack is extravagantly, inordinately coloured: the reds are blood red—spilling over the edges; the ace of spades blacker than the riding boots of the Earl of Hell; the court cards are far more courtly than usual, the royal faces more regal, the knaves more knavish, the whole design more devious. And of course Romance is far more Romantic for there is always that card at the end of the pack with a picture of a red rose on it and the ageless legend beneath: 'Rudolph—Flavia—Always.'

The cards marked 'Fact' in our minds are no less gaudy, bloody and adventurous: we see a vastly mixed pugnacious race of Turks, Greeks, Slavs, Romanians and a dozen other factions—fighting it out back and forth through history in an isolated mountainous corner of Europe, but particularly at war with each other between about 1870 and 1914: the Macedonian Question, the Treaty of San Stefano, the Congress of Berlin, the Serbian Problem and finally Sarajevo, the Archduke Ferdinand and a piece of paper in 1914: that day in Bosnia where all the cards—the courtly figures and the knaves, the facts and the fiction—came together and went up in a puff of smoke, a smell of gunpowder on the breeze that became a holocaust as it spread through Europe. The Balkans then, like the Middle-East today, was the powder keg that finally exploded. How apt the cartoonist's symbol of it all was: the anarchist's bomb, round like a plum pudding with its crackling fuse—a perfect link between the reality and the fiction of those times.

That Edwardian era seems to lie at the heart of our imaginative response to the Balkans. We are looking through the glass of history, or reading one of Anthony Hope's turn of the century Ruritanian novels, and we are immediately transported into a world of high adventure and low politics; of sacrifice, passion, heroism, evil—all on the grandest possible scale; stories—or facts—of deceived Kings, unscrupulous Queens, fair Princesses and disinherited Princes; of rascally uncles—provincial warlords lurking in the mountains about to march on the capital; of diplomatic emissaries—wily Germans, French and Italians, together with high-minded British officers and gentlemen—all none the less equally set on furthering their own great power causes: the continentals through bribery, seduction and such like, the British by more subtle ruses, ideally involving their disguise as butterfly collectors, trout fishermen or Serbian peasants. And then—so often a part of this Balkan tableau—the lower orders: serfs, shopkeepers, valets and chambermaids, whose star can rise so fortuitously in these fictional kingdoms, or by whose actions—a rope ladder left over the moat at midnight —the whole story is changed utterly, just as in historical fact in those real Balkan kingdoms, the same sort of underdogs—students, teachers and mild-mannered civil servants—brought about even more dramatic change with that plum pudding bomb and its fizzing fuse.

Are we in Sarajevo that August day by the river in 1914, with the assassin Princip and his other hapless, idealistic friends, waiting for the Archduke's car to pass? Or are we in Slavna, that imaginary capital in Anthony Hope's *Sophy of Kravonia* waiting in the palace with the dead King for the English kitchen-maid and her Prince to attack at dawn? Sometimes it's difficult to tell where we are. The fact and the fiction become confused, interchangeable. Sometimes, indeed, the fiction can completely override the facts and become more real than any historical or geographical reality.

Graham Greene has written of this feeling, talking of the first film he ever saw—the same *Sophy of Kravonia*. 'It was a story that captured me forever,' he writes. 'The Balkans since have always been Kravonia—the area of infinite possibility, and it was through the mountains of Kravonia that I drove a few summers ago and not through the Carpathians of my Atlas. That was the kind of book I always wanted to write: the high romantic tale, capturing us in youth with hopes that prove illusions, to which we return again in age in order to escape the sad reality.'

Most of us nurture one of these imaginary kingdoms in our hearts—an 'area of infinite possibility', a kingdom often induced by some imaginative youthful experience—a book, a film, a nursery fable. And for me the Balkans became just a place, a realm of endless drama and romance. And my particular vision of the area, a strange amalgam of fact and fancy, started with a film too.

Years ago, in Bath, in a tiny cinema in an alley-way near the Abbey, I first saw *The Lady Vanishes*. It was a dead Sunday afternoon in February, the middle of one of the coldest winters ever, and the snow had piled up against the wall outside the cinema partly covering the old production stills of Margaret Lockwood, Michael Redgrave, Basil Radford and Naunton Wayne.

And once inside, and the film had started with those images of a similarly snow-bound world, a small car moving silently through the crisp drifts on the alpine village square, I was hooked. I had started on that imaginative journey, a peculiar mental transference from the facts of a snow-bound winter in Bath to the fantasy of one in the Balkans. And very shortly, of course, that other great fictional prop—equal to any in Anthony Hope's Ruritania—that clattering, glittering symbol of all Balkan adventure, took over the film: the express train journey.

The Lady Vanishes, Stamboul Train, Murder on the Orient Express—these, and other books, and the Hitchcock film seen again, linked the Balkans with express trains indelibly in my mind. That cut-off world of irresponsible movement, watching a foreign spring come up from a train window vanishing south-wards—the waiters swaying down the restaurant car balancing drinks trays, a message from the obsequious wagon-lit attendant, the tall woman crying in the Athens slip coach—all these became essential ingredients in an essential means of travel towards that area of infinite possibility. And I had taken the Orient Express through the Balkans many times with Hercule Poirot, pursuing the mysterious Miss Froy and Greene's sad schoolteacher revolutionary Dr. Cziner, before I ever went there in reality. And if there was an epicentre to my fantasy, a precise spot on my fictional map of the Balkans where all these images coalesced, it came at that moment at the end of *The Lady Vanishes* where the rival factions shoot it out in a snowy forest glade in the middle of nowhere: the gallant English in tweeds, with pipes and one revolver in the wagon-lit against the evil militia in great coats, sharply peaked caps with Jackboots touting lugers from behind every tree. It haunted me sometimes—the exact whereabouts of that snow-filled forest which Michael Redgrave walked away into, dispensing final justice. Where was it? The place must surely exist somewhere in the Balkans, one part of me said, so convinced was I by the illusion. But afterwards the facts took over again, the 'sad reality' that Greene spoke of, and I knew that the snowy glade, the wagon-lit, the tweeds, the pipes and the lugers had never been anything more than props set up on the back lot at Sheperton studios.

Such was the rag-bag of facts and fancies that I took with me to Messrs. Thomas Cook in Berkeley Street earlier this year, ordering a first-class wagon-lit return on the Orient Express: Paris–Bucharest–Paris, via Zagreb, Belgrade and Sofia.

Of course as far as my fancies went it was a doomed journey from the beginning. I realized that—or one part of me did. I'd been on the tatty, overcrowded Orient Express once before as far as Zagreb; I'd lived in Tito's Yugoslavia for several months and I'd done my homework on the post-war communist regimes of Bulgaria and Romania. It is, to me, one of history's considerable ironies that the Balkan people, for so long the epitome of rash adventure and individual spirit should, in the space of a genera- tion, have become so completely dominated by a political system ruthlessly opposed to all such idiosyncratic characteristics. The transformation has all the strangeness, carries all the shock and insult, of a fairy story ending badly—*Sophy of Kravonia* or *The Lady Vanishes* culminating in despair—as if Hitchcock had made an insane mistake in shooting the end of that film, having the militia storm the wagon-lit, and, in a last frozen frame, the lugers covering them, left the adventurous travellers stalled in silence ever since.

Yes, one part of me knew that Marx and Lenin had sup- planted Anthony Hope and Agatha Christie in the Balkans. Yet there was still another tiny part of me that travelled hopefully. And when I woke on my first morning out of Paris to a tray of confiture and coffee, and saw the alps and the Italian lakes flash by outside the wagon-lit window, I thought, my goodness, perhaps it's all really going to be all right in the end. Any moment now the attendant would be tapping on my door—would I come please?—there was a tall woman crying in the Athens slip coach . . .

It's a truism, of course, that the Orient Express is not what it was. But I was not prepared for the truism to become a joke, as it did after we left Milan. From there on the 'express' becomes nothing more than a short haul commuter train for suburban Italian business men and a long-distance cattle wagon for hordes of returning Greek and Yugoslav emigrant workers from West Germany. As well, as if in preparation for the oncoming communist austerity, the train sheds every luxury—buffet cars, everything. Nothing was left as we drew out of Milan station except one very shabby wagon-lit, three first-class compartments and enough chianti and salami in the other fifteen carriages to repeat the miracle of the loaves and fishes.

We crawled all afternoon across the northern Italian plain, stopped at every Venetian suburb, never had a glimpse even of the lido or lagoons, reversed out again at nightfall and meandered endlessly towards Trieste—then Sezana, the Yugoslav frontier station, where we stopped for an hour while all the Greeks and Turks in the train were evicted to get transit visas. The Yugoslavs are very border conscious these days. 'It not ever happens to me before,' a well-travelled Greek from Cardiff, of all places, told me nervously as he climbed down onto the rails in pitch darkness, a light snow beginning to fall, small white pin-pricks against the carriage windows, slanting quickly against the glass in a bitter wind that had come up with the night. And again I felt a sudden glow of hope, leaning out the window for a moment, the snow tingling and then melting on my scalp. At last a bit of proper Balkan weather, I thought. Soon there'd be the real thing: snow drifts further down the line and fast taxis to Belgrade. And the frontier station was very much up to form too: border guards with machine-pistols, officious customs men searching every stick of luggage, lines of shabby, tired passengers waiting for their transit visas in the cold yellow station lights and, like one of those sinister transformations in *Alice in Wonderland*, a whole new set of train officials who had sud-

denly taken over, crept up on us all unawares—no longer the
slick Italian volubility, but now a group of silent strong-faced
men in greatcoats and red stars on their sharply peaked caps . . .

Ah yes, I thought, this is better—much better. I got my own
heavy coat down from the rack. The half bottle of cognac I'd got
at Milan was still there—and the two salami rolls and the
orange. That should just see us through the snow drifts in the
taxi—myself and the tall woman who had stopped crying in
the Athens slip coach.

When I got off at Zagreb it was 2.30 in the morning, the
station deserted and it was spilling with rain. I carried my heavy
bags out into the forecourt looking for a taxi. There weren't
any. They were on strike. Instead there was an advertisement in
the station buffet window, the rain weeping down across a plum
brandy bottle, the name 'Badel' in smudged lettering underneath. 'Badel, Slivovica'. I looked at the sign carefully. It meant
everything—and nothing. What in God's name was I doing here
face to face with this advertisement in the soaking forecourt of
Zagreb station at 2.30 on a winter's morning—a thousand-mile
journey just to meet a piece of coloured cardboard in a buffet
window? And just as there had been unreasonable hope hours
before, with dreams of snow and crazy Serbian taxi-drivers, now
there was irrational anger at this drab appointment, seemingly
predestined—that low moment in travel when all the reasons
fail and one is left clutching nothing but a ticket, now seen at
last for what it always was, a confidence trick, a lure to a happy
land from a fraudulent siren, an old hag.

Yet I had at least one reason for stopping off at Zagreb.
Twenty years before, on a holiday exchange, a summer just
coming up to autumn before I went back to school, I'd fallen in
love with a girl here, seventeen, the daughter of a doctor, with
rings of fair hair done up like a vol-au-vent case around her head,
a turned-up nose and a great look of scandalized merriment
about the eyes. I thought I might look her up again.

She'd lived on the far side of Strossmayer Square, the long
leafy park with its fountains and heroic statues that runs right
through the centre of the old Hapsburg city. 'Little Vienna'
Zagreb used to be known as—the blue trams clanking in the
sunlight beneath the huge plane trees which I travelled in on
every afternoon from the suburbs to see the girl.

Next to the entrance to her parent's apartment was a small workers' buffet, the door swinging open all the time, like a fan, wafting plum brandy out onto the air. And since it was nearly autumn then, there was—as outside most other apartment blocks in the city centre—a little machine-saw humming on the pavement, two men cutting beech-wood into neat logs for the green porcelain stoves upstairs, and I'd rise to meet the girl with sawdust in my hair and rumours of plum and resin in my nose.

We always had tea together with her parents at five o'clock, rather formally with petit fours and Earl Grey's best Darjeeling sent out from the Army & Navy Stores. Then I'd go out with her, very innocently—rowing on the lakes at the Zoo, a cinema for a shilling, or blow five shillings on the terrace of the Gradski Kavana on lemon ices, or sometimes for a penny we'd take the cable car up to the old town on the hill looking over the city and wander round the mediaeval Kaptol with its miniature parks, huge sudden views, its narrow streets, plump churches and candle-lit street shrines. It was one of those kind of summers.

Why not look her up, I thought next morning. Probably married, but her parents would surely be around. But they weren't in the 'phone book. So I wandered across Strossmayer square, the naked plane trees whipped by a bitter wind now and a fine sleet, and down the side street to the huge doorway of the block where they'd all lived. The stucco was cracking all over the outside of it and the hallway was battered and dirty as it never had been, the mail boxes off their hinges—and no, a woman told me on the first floor landing which had been theirs —no one, no doctor of that name had ever lived there.

'A girl,' I said, giving her name.

'No,' the woman said. 'There's a doctor in one room on the ground floor. But he isn't married.'

'But there must have been,' I said. I could see the green porcelain stove in the hallway of the flat that I'd remembered, and a neat pile of the same wood beside it.

'That stove—I remember—'

'There are many such stoves in Zagreb,' the woman said distrustfully, and she closed the door.

The young doctor was at home and he spoke English. He was extremely cordial.

'But,' he said, 'Your friends never lived here. I know the

name, never met them. They live in the next block, down the street, number 17. Easy to make a mistake, identical blocks.'

When I got to number 17 I found that the entire doorway had been carefully bricked up. But there were lights on in all the windows of the building, the sound of typewriters. The whole place had been turned into some kind of government office, with its entrance further down along the street. There was a van parked outside. They were carrying in a lot of files and filing cabinets.

'No,' the porter told me inside, the building had been converted, had been part of the Ministry for more than twenty years. No one had lived here since the war.

It was very cold now and I walked back to speak to the young doctor again. But he wasn't in this time. I left the building and then I saw it; I'd forgotten it, hadn't noticed it before: the little workers' buffet just along from their block that had reeked of plum brandy that summer. I'd come to the right place first time round.

There was another man I'd known then, who'd known the doctor's family too. He'd been the representative for a foreign business and had had his office in the Palace Hotel on the other side of the square. Perhaps he'd know what had happened to them. I remembered his suite of rooms in the old Strauss-style hotel with its gilded ceilings, chandeliers, cherubs and mirrors, and talks we'd had there about bee-keeping of all things.

The hotel was still there. But inside it was unrecognizable—a harsh, arid decor, tubular steel everywhere and a smell of some kind of synthetic lavender. And no, the manager said, no one of that name had ever had an office in the hotel and the firm itself had always had its agency in Republic square. Perhaps if I saw them they could help . . .

I didn't bother. Instead I went out to the man's house in the suburbs that afternoon and a huge woman shouted at me from an upstairs window.

'He doesn't live here,' she bellowed.

'But he *did*.'

'No—he never lived here.'

My Serbo-Croatian wasn't good enough to argue. She knew his name, I thought, but *he* had never lived here.

It was like Kafka, or the beginning of another *Lady Vanishes*

I thought. Yet it wasn't fiction; it was all perfectly real, I knew, when I got to Zagreb station next morning to pick up the Orient Express again, and I found myself looking at the plum brandy advertisement in the buffet window. 'Badel Slivovica'. It meant everything—and nothing.

6

Here be Dragons

[June 1974]

By the time we'd got to the last station before the Bulgarian frontier almost all the passengers in the Orient Express had left the train. It had been packed out at Belgrade with an extraordinary collection, as varied as a travelling circus, who'd rushed the train from all sides across the shallow platforms: heavily whiskered Serbian farmers in great-boots, tunics and soiled astrakhans, and their small, goblin-faced wives in shawls and fifty billowing petticoats going back to their villages after a day's shopping in the capital; collections of smart-suited young men in kipper ties and flared pants going home to the same villages for the week-end to impress the girls—playing squeaky Macedonian music full volume on transistors and constantly combing their hair. And there were those others—grey faced, indeterminate men in crinkled suits with old briefcases, a bad stubble and spit in the corners of their lips—that one always comes across travelling in European trains. They haven't any luggage and they sit by themselves and sleep with their shoes off, their feet on a copy of a week old copy of the *Corriere della Sera*. Who are they? Where are they going? Anyway, apart from these silent travellers, there had been that Balkan railway frenzy at Belgrade station, so reminiscent of journeys in India— a football match on all the platforms, of shouting and pushing and people stumbling over huge straw-bound demi-johns of wine. And when the whistle went and the kissing had to stop there was that marvellous moment, like watching the start of a race, when everyone decided to get on the moving train at the same moment: stout men jumping like gazelles for the nearest door and thin ones sprinting up the platform for another access further up. I pulled an old couple up myself, fat and heavy they were, landing them like big carp on the floor of the corridor, while the train was really moving. And you could hear the shouting and the weeping on the platform, from the old mothers

157

and lovers and brothers and sisters and husbands and wives left behind—all behaving dreadfully, as if the train had been a boat for America.

And this mood of high emotionalism continued for most of the journey as the train crawled eastwards through the mountain gorges: people singing and drinking and weeping, lining the corridors, dancing in the compartments—with just those lonely mysterious men, cut off from it all, staring woefully out in the black afternoon at the impoverished cottages on the sides of the hills, the sky lowering all the time and the wind cutting in from the Russian north more and more bitterly as the evening came. The carriage lights went on. There were more rounds of drink. Peals of sudden laughter. And the squeaky music was so loud now that you couldn't hear the wheels groaning as the huge train rounded the endless curves of the valley. A farmer crooked a straw-covered demi-john of red wine on his elbow, missed his friend's glass, and the liquid streaked all over the corridor window. The train had become a moveable feast, a long party, self-contained, raucous, a glittering snake twisting through the night.

And then, one by one, at two or three stations before the Bulgarian border, all the carriages emptied, people falling down on the rails shouting 'Zhivio' and 'Laku noce', spitting thoroughly and stumbling home through the snow that had started to fall, a thin white dust covering the shallow platforms, the wind rising, whipping the petticoats of the old women and tossing the hair of the smart drunken young men and drowning all their squeaky music.

We went across the border, the party over, the train terribly quiet. And when we got to Dragoman, the Bulgarian frontier station, the snow was really tumbling down, carpeting and silencing everything. We waited here for a long while. And I noticed two raggedey gypsy children outside my window, very young and barefoot, collecting coke bottles along the tracks in the snow. They wore short nightdresses over their billowy pantaloons—the same arab *galibeah's* that children wear in Egypt—and their faces were thin, the eyes set very deep and dark, their hair cropped right back to the skull, and they skipped around in the snowy wind like white flappy animals from out of the nearby woods. A fairy tale. A magic carpet.

Something Arabian had passed in the night. A desert had touched the snow. Then a group of frontier officials got on board. And I could hear them a long way off tramping up the deserted carriages towards me.

I've never had such a clear or eerie impression of changing countries, passing from one society to another, from laughter to silence, of arriving somewhere at midnight in the snow, a frontier station that leads to a land where the maps run out. And the white weather coming down like a lid on the world seemed a portent of everything to come.

If Yugoslav communism is the most enterprising and free-wheeling among the Eastern bloc nations, the Bulgarian version is the most egalitarian and monolithic. It's the basic hard core variety here, almost Stalinist. Though none of this is really apparent to the hundreds of thousands of western tourists who flock out the Black Sea resorts every year now. Golden Sands and Sunny Beach are a long way from Sofia. And the tourists live in sunny ghettos, completely isolated, specially built holiday communities, which ordinary Bulgarians are not allowed use. Bulgaria is more cut off from the West than any other Eastern bloc nation. Western books and newspapers are strictly unavailable—as is travel abroad for 99.99 per cent of the citizenry. The Bulgarian news media, together with the arts, have been so rigidly controlled for so long that the party has actually had to sponsor a satiric weekly magazine along with a satiric theatre, to promote acceptable jokes at the expense of laggardly workers and factory managers late with their five-year plans. And the same is true of pop groups: since the party can't proscribe transistors with the stomping and wailing from Belgrade and Vienna, it trains its own combos, through the Folklore and Youth committees in every town, and sends them out complete with electric guitars and fairly long hair to sing more decorously and less stridently—words of lost love and all that, certainly, but set in some appropriate Marxist context. I heard some of this music and I liked it a lot. Easy on the ear and very restful. And some of it has become genuinely popular.

In Bulgaria the party clamped down after the war and has remained completely in control and almost totally unmoving ever since. A whole generation of Bulgarians have grown up without ever hearing about the West or apparently noticing even a rumble of the communist dissension elsewhere in the Eastern bloc. There has never been a thaw here: Kruschev, Hungary, Czechoslovakia—all came and went without an echo in these parts.

Bulgaria, both politically and geographically, must, next to Albania, be the most isolated country in Europe. Here be Dragons indeed. And you feel this, strongly, the moment you cross over the border. For me it was an eye-opener, this first experience of so rigidly controlled a society, such a dogmatic communism.

Party Secretary Todor Zhivkov and his senior colleagues have come so completely to dominate affairs, feel so secure in their positions and their policies so unassailable, that there is an extraordinary sense of peaceful other worldliness in Bulgaria, especially in Sofia—a feeling of being in a bowl along with the goldfish yet not being a goldfish oneself. The people swim round you. But they are looking through you. They do not see you. Western assumptions have very little meaning here at all. The concept of the individual seems non-existent. And nobody on the surface seems any the worse off for it. Rather the opposite. They like it. They seem to thrive on it. The Bulgarians have always had a reputation for hard work, discipline, seriousness. They are supremely unfrivolous by nature. And this form of immobile despotic paternalism seems to suit them very well. Everyone gets on with his thing. There are no alternatives. The word has disappeared from their dictionaries. That whole slice of life which deals with the larger choices and decisions has been removed from them, as if by lobotomy. And the populace, so successfully corralled from every other world, is not aware of this loss and are thus happier than most of us are. They can relax.

One of the most pleasing things about Sofia is the lack of big city bustle and tension. It has a population of more than a million. But apart from the rush hours or the frenzy induced by the arrival of some miniature Russian TV sets in one of the State shops, Sofia is as peaceful and orderly a place as Chipping Campden. Another pleasant fact was the almost complete absence—so unlike the other satellite nations—of any police, secret or otherwise. Of course they exist, but because there is no threat to the regime, internal or external, there is no need for the police to be *seen* to exist. They are back at the station playing chess or servicing the cobwebby eavesdropping machinery. For, apart from the embassies, there's little need for that in Bulgaria either. Beyond a teacher or two, there are no foreigners living in Sofia, no Western correspondents or press agencies, and only a very few Western commercial enterprises, represented part time by agents flying in from Vienna or Bucharest every month or so.

Among the Bulgarians themselves there's no need for microphones either. It was my strong feeling that unlike the Romanians and Yugoslavs they were genuinely ignorant or uninterested in democratic alternatives and quite unaware of any contradiction in the endless party manifestos, advertisements and general spiel about peace and happiness through Marx and the wickedness of everything in the West. Brainwashed? No, I don't think so. There was never any need for this. Marxism was an acceptable cult from the beginning for this desperately impoverished, feudal country. The Russians, by and large, are liked—and for good reason, since they liberated the Bulgarians both from the Turks and the Nazis. There are very strong racial and linguistic ties between the two people; economically Bulgaria has done very well out of the association. They are genuinely grateful to the Russians. No one is going to rock the boat in Bulgaria for the ship of state was never made to float at all. It lies far up the shore, bolted down, behind glass, correct in every ideological detail.

This strange peace, this orderly flatulence—Orwellian in flavour—is most apparent in the middle of Sofia, where I stayed at the Grand Balkan Hotel, surrounded by immense mid-'Fifties Stalinist government buildings, made of granite blocks the size of cottages. The streets in this area are very wide, yellow-cobbled and are banned to traffic. They are so clean that to drop a match as I did on my first morning, is to be stared at and made to feel— quite rightly—a considerable pig. Dark-suited men from the Ministries in minute brown homburgs move silently to and fro across these huge perspectives, together with army officers marching eyes front in ankle-length greatcoats with briefcases as if on parade. Ordinary citizens quicken their pace through this quarter. To loiter is not forbidden in these huge quadrangles. But there is the sense in doing so that someone in one of the thousands of windows above has begun to take an undue interest in you. So no one stops and chatters.

But they do all this, and more, in the Grand Balkan Hotel round the corner. This magnificence, though built in the 'Fifties, is Edwardian in its exaggerated scale, its heavy pomposity and art nouveau decor. The hall is as big as half a football pitch in polished marble, the stairway like a direct access to God, with huge ballrooms and countless foyers and salons giving of it everywhere. And in these endless ante-rooms I have never seen such feasting, feeding, drinking, toasting—at dances, weddings, receptions. It went on round the clock—from the day I arrived until my departure five days later. I left the hotel at noon one day, passing a salon on the first floor next my bedroom and, its being International Women's Week that week in the Marxian calendar, a huge clutch of attractive women (and the Bulgarian women are very attractive) had just arrived and were embarking on a lot of neat Rakia. I got back at seven o'clock and passed the door again. There was the sound of bagpipe music and cheering. A piece of furniture fell over. I longed for a peep inside. I tiptoed over and tried the door handle. It was firmly locked—on the inside.

Two inter-related factors of social life in Bulgaria were made very apparent in the Grand Balkan Hotel—both the result of an isolated, and utterly confident and intensely conservative party ideology. The first was the extreme propriety of all public intercourse. Barring the ladies with the bagpipes, the mood throughout these receptions, lunch parties, weddings and *thé dansants*, in rooms behind heavy velvet drapes with potted plants beneath great chandeliers, was, of course, precisely Edwardian; as were the trappings—the gilded decor, the gold lamé dresses of the women, the men really stuffing out their shirts, the immensely elaborate place layings with a dozen implements and four different-sized wineglasses, unsuitable mounds of flowers at intervals, champagne coolers everywhere; the endless toasting and speeches longer still—all this very formal, confident, yet slightly vulgar show could have been taken straight from a banquet of rich milliners and grocers at the Imperial Hotel, Russell square, in 1910.

Almost every item in my bedroom, from the bedside light to the lavatory cistern, could have come straight out of an old

Army & Navy Stores' catalogue. And of course it was all very comfortable and reassuring. Is this the simple reason for it all? Reassurance for the new class of privileged party members who have been so suddenly catapulted either from serfdom before the war, or from a factory floor, into exposed social positions—and thus have to protect themselves, hiding their lack of any really felt manners, through these endless formalities and toastings, just as those merchants did aping high society in the London of 1910. Marvellous irony, of course, that the original communist revolution should have been dedicated to overthrowing just such a class and destroying all such bourgeois appendages. Yet nothing could have been so robustly bourgeois, or could have better confirmed the existence of Djilas' 'New Class', than the society of the Grand Balkan Hotel—the day-long partying, yet so stilted, the guests so timeless in their greedy expectation, their mammoth fulfilment.

The other factor behind these huge group receptions—and it's equally apparent in the streets, cafés, restaurants and offices in Sofia—is the herd instinct. People rarely do things in ones or twos but in groups of five, ten or a dozen. Walking, eating, talking, shopping, giving an interview—there is always a *crowd* involved. This gregariousness might seem at first evidence simply of a warm humanity. But it is much more a protective ploy, a camouflage, a means of survival in a fiercely regimented society, and as such inevitably entails a sacrifice of individual identity and a loss of many essentially human qualities.

I've said I thought the Bulgarians were reasonably happy with their hard lot—and they are, on a conscious, rational level. They have made a go of things; they have survived—and are surviving —psychological and physical pressures which would be unimaginable in the West. But the efforts expended on this have drained the people of their social equilibrium, their emotional repose. So many people one meets at a professional level in Sofia are strangely and slightly off-key in everything they do: their behaviour is minutely frenzied in committing even the smallest, most ordinary act of initiative—like making a 'phone call. They have been told for so long that someone else, for the good of all, is finally in charge: the Party—remote, all-seeing, wise. Destiny belongs entirely in the public sector. There is a Ministry of Destiny with many servants attached. It is not a private thing

any more. And while the people consciously accept this as a fact
of life necessary for their survival, they resent it in other less
conscious ways, which makes them edgy and unconfident in
their personal affairs. Their behaviour is a small but crucial
degree out of true. The gap between the Party's demands and
private wishes, between reality and themselves, is widening all
the time. A mild schizophrenia is evident everywhere—hence
the desire to herd whenever possible. For to get together, formally or in cafés, is both to conform, not to be seen as someone
outside the group, and to be reminded, however symbolically, of
an undivided, confident humanity which is seeping from their
daily lives.

Celebration in Bulgaria is a serious business. It is not oblivion
the people seek but a guiltless balance between the public and
their private world, a personal release within the safety of the
crowd. Those rakias and wineglasses, the champagne coolers
and Strauss music, the crammed restaurants and cafés—all are
an offering for future survival, mental and physical; they are
not part of any present laughter or past memories.

There is a poem by one of the best of their writers, Elissaveta
Bagryana, which sums up the present Bulgarian mood very well
—its stoicism, its discipline, rationalism, its acceptance of things
as they are, and yet the sense of personal loss that all these hard-
won virtues have entailed:

> I've got everything I need
> to live:
> a home, modest, but my own,
> I have no debts . . .
> I am loved by my relatives.
> and friends, I hope.
> I am in good health,
> considering my age.
> Sometimes I travel—
> perhaps not as much as I'd like to,
> perhaps not where I would like to,
> but so many others
> haven't got even that.
> I have plenty of time.
> On the face of it

there's nothing standing in the way
of my art.
But more and more often of late
my heart's been gripped by sorrow,
my power and will
are paralysed . . .
I do my best
to fight them back
with my reason,
but the sleepless nights . . .
    No, no!
I am not unhappy,
but to be unhappy,
and not to be happy
are two different things . . .

7

Sleeper to Bucharest

[June 1974]

Where the Bulgarians, with Slav stoicism, generally accept the communist reality, the Romanians, a Latin race, are always trying to beat the system. The Bulgarian political line is indistinguishable from Moscow's; they are terrified of western influence. The Romanians, on a 600-mile border with the Soviet Union, fear Russia and court the West. You notice the difference in attitudes on the Orient Express. On the Bulgarian sector, an overnight wagon-lit sleeper from Sofia to Bucharest was £1.50 extra. From Bucharest to Belgrade you were right back with the profit motives of the capitalist West: the identical overnight sleeper was £10 extra.

Romania is still temperamentally a Latin province. But the roads to Rome have long since vanished and for centuries it has been an embattled island, overrun and occupied time and again, by Turks, Slavs, Russians and Germans. The Romanians are reeds who've learnt to bend with every wind, pragmatists, adept in all the most cunning arts of survival. They are the Irish of the Balkans who've long ago learnt to tell you what you'd like to hear rather than the truth of the matter. For them life is *la bella figura*: the real plans go on all the time behind the colour and the dash of the apparently real. They are volatile, devious, imaginative, theatrical; they are chatterboxes, drive like fiends, and would like nothing better than to while their lives away at a café table in the sun.

Unfortunately history has brought them to a worker's canteen. They are seated, of course—they had little choice—over their meagre fare. And after lunch they fill their quota for the greater glory of all the Marxist Gods. But by evening they have changed roles dramatically. They are back in town strolling the corso en masse, and packing out the beer halls and cafés and red plush restaurants over steak tartare. After work they go back over a temperamental border into the West.

166

And this mental adaptability, this history of expediency, of doing one thing but thinking another, is exactly reflected in Romania's current political ambitions. Here they walk a non-aligned tightrope, with Moscow lurking on the left, the West on the right, pursuing as independent a policy as they dare, making friends in the West as fast as they decently can, while always assuring the Soviet Union of their basic commitment to every Marxist-Leninist principle. It's a perilous performance which Party Secretary Nicolae Ceausesku handles with great skill, though at the cost of any real liberal adventure at home. For in order to persuade the Russians of his good intentions towards them, and to give them no excuse for military intervention, Ceausesku has had to maintain a very rigid domestic security, a close surveillance of all those Romanian virtues of initiative and individuality which make up their *bella figura*. Because of this life on the surface in Romania is far more visibly controlled than it is in hard line Bulgaria. Romanians suffer an awkward paradox as a result of their non-alignment, for to make any liberal experiment with Marxism requires more secret police than simply to maintain a genuinely repressive version of the creed. The Romanian communist party, though not essentially repressive at all, must at times be seen to be so, with the result that grocers and factory managers are shot from time to time for embezzlement, while the party never ceases to exhort and impose the most stringent socialist principles on the populace.

Thus the country lives by two different standards: a hard official code and a lax private one. And the people, unlike the Bulgarians, are perfectly well aware of this dualism and how to live with it. As long as there is no open conflict between these public and private worlds, the Party tolerates, or turns a blind eye, to the expression of all those Romanian virtues of dash and independence, for it knows that its tightrope act is finally dependent on fostering the people's sense of nationalism and adventure.

Indeed, without successfully maintaining this spirit, Ceausesku would be in trouble at home, for Romanians are not much given to heroism, or great ideals, to put it mildly, and they prefer to keep clear of people who have dared and failed in these matters. Romanians have had their doubts about Ceausesku's independent line; it is Ceausesku who rocks the boat in Romania—some of the crew wish the ship had never left port.

Because of this dualism—the existence of an adventurous party on one hand, and of a wily Latin citizenry on the other—life in Bucharest is very deceptive. On the surface, with its ubiquitous leather-coated plainclothesmen, its endless tales of bugging, blackmail and blondes in your bedroom, the place has all the trappings of a vigorous police state. Yet one immediately notices things which would be impossible if such were really the case: Western books, plays, films, as well as Western newspapers freely available in the big hotels, along with Romanian cultural offerings of considerable unorthodoxy, such as a recent 'Hamlet' where the court at Elsinore, corrupted by the uncle, is clearly meant to draw a parallel with Soviet designs on Romania; above all, in the week I was there, which suddenly turned into a winter heat wave, the sensuous *joie de vivre* of life in Bucharest, as the people massed outdoors at cafés for the first time of the year, swilling litres of white wine and soda—all this seemed incompatable with the equally clear impressions of surveïllance and orthodoxy which I drew from the city. But the Romanians have reconciled these opposites: the reed bends with one wind, and then with another: tempting spring breeze or angry winter storm: hock and seltzer or the next five-year plan—they pay equal tribute to both.

This worldliness behind the mask of orthodox communist dogma was perfectly apparent, even during the many official interviews I had in Bucharest. Whereas in Bulgaria I felt sure that each civil servant I spoke to really believed his piece about peace and happiness through Marx and Lenin, it was clear that Romanian officials, who never failed to say *exactly* the same thing to me, did not altogether believe in this gospel, if they believed it at all. No hint of this apostasy ever passed their lips. But it was obvious in their faces, their tone; they were not to be deceived—though they hoped I would be. And senior officials, sure of their position and with the ear of Ceausesku, would sometimes openly contradict and condemn what I'd been told by junior people in the same Union or Ministry. Such variance in the text given a foreign journalist would have been unthinkable in Sofia.

Once you appreciate these contradictions life in Bucharest suddenly makes sense. A flying visit, with all those leather-coated men, could well put you off. But with a full week strolling around the place, luck with friends and with a sharp eye, one sees how many irreconcilables have been cleverly brought together while some party official's back was turned. The essence of it all—and the Party is perfectly aware of this—is that to be happy, Romanians, and the Bucharesti in particular, must express themselves in some individual and therefore usually illicit way.

Thus moonlighting—two, three and more jobs at a time—is common, as is petty corruption of all kinds—bribing party officials to ensure that one's children are not packed off to the provinces at the start of their careers being one of the most common forms of it. And Bucharest is one of those nice places where almost everything can be 'fixed'—from the gear box on your pre-war Ford saloon, to obtaining suitable placement for your son-in-law in the Ministry of Rest and Recreation.

The gear boxes, along with a great many other finicky old-fashioned mechanical contrivances, are handled in a number of privately-owned little shops in the old city—down Moshilor and Coltea streets, a marvellous narrow warren where all sorts of artisans work in dark cubby-holes next the pavement. Furriers and second-hand clothes merchants predominate, with aspidistras in the windows, flanking decaying mountain hares and silver foxes, their eyes and teeth alone still in good shape, gleaming and snapping malevolently. And in the next shop a row of genuine tenth-hand Oxford bags in the window, very old and shiny and hard pressed, together with white-and-brown co-respondent's shoes and cracked dancing pumps. Clothes that had survived so much, I thought, remembering those school essays in which one had to write 'The Autobiography of a Shilling'. The original owners must have long since perished, little over-confident men with sleek-brilliantined scalps, commercial travellers in the Bucharest of the 'Thirties, who had seen the latest fashion ads from London or Paris, or who had travelled to Berlin and had come back to these very same tailor's shops to ape the ways of the West. And the shops had stayed the same—through the European holocaust: the bombing of Bucharest, the purges, transportations, the concentration camps; King Carol and Madame Lupescu, Hitler and Anna Pauker had come and gone. And Marx and Lenin were here now. But it had all made no

difference; the trousers would still serve another turn. To look in
these windows was to thumb through an Army & Navy Stores'
catalogue for 1929. And it's a common Proustian experience,
this, under socialism, for one saw just the same sort of shops in
the back streets of Sofia. It seems that only under a communist
regime, with its great scarcity of choice and individual service,
can such small artisan's shops survive. And with them the
Oxford bags, the old Ford gear boxes and the 1930's Gillette
razors—the minutae, the bric-à-brac which was our past as well.
And there is the irony again—that Marxism, destroying the
society which created these passing fads and fancies, should now
be the only system to preserve and find a use for these little
emblems of capitalism.

On my last morning in Bucharest I went out to the suburbs
to visit Dr. Ana Aslan's famous Institute of Geriatrics, where
the elderly—and the young at heart—come from all over the
world at £15 a day for a dose of her patent Gerovital H-3 treatment—and from where, in return, the good professor leaves to
visit such ideologically opposed notables as Peron and Chairman
Mao with her little bottles of the magic elixir. By all accounts
the patients enjoy it all and benefit from it—for ageing is an
idea as much as a physical process, and to be treated solicitously
and expensively for the complaint in exotic Bucharest would be
to feel younger at once, I should have thought. However, the
only reliable evidence as yet to show that the mixture works
lies in experiments they conduct at the clinic—with rats.

I started this Balkan journey with thoughts of mystery and
adventure, the old image of the area, the fictional image of the
'Thirties thriller: *Stamboul Train, Murder on the Orient Express*
and above all *The Lady Vanishes*. And I was pleased that at the
very end of my journey through the often drab reality of these
lands, I should come across still remaining evidence of that spirit
of mystery and derring-do, a perfect setting for one of those
pre-war thrillers—for the clinic I got to that morning might
well have been the place that poor Miss Froy was destined for
until Michael Redgrave so bravely intervened.

The Lady Vanishes. And she could well have vanished here,
into this huge nineteenth-century fortress of a building, up a
long drive, surrounded by stumpy winter trees and elderly
withered couples moving painfully along the gravel paths in

slippers and dressing-gowns. Dr. Aslan was away but although I had a firm appointment there was no one to meet me and no one who knew anything about me. The long corridors were deserted. I was shown to a waiting-room on the first floor. A blonde woman and a suave man were deep in conversation with notebooks at a table but they stopped as soon as I came in. They looked at me curiously and then resumed their notes in silence. Suddenly a lift started downstairs, the machinery cranking and whirring upwards. Then it stopped. The gates clanged and a man like Toulouse Lautrec popped into the waiting-room. He wore a beret, a waxy white coat and a pair of pin-stripe morning trousers. He was in charge of the experiments with the rats.

'Oh yes,' I said. 'I'd like to see that.'

I'd said it without thinking. I didn't really want to see the rats at all. We walked a long way, out to an annexe behind the building. I heard a twittering, like thousands of birds in a tree and I looked up. But there were no trees, just high walls. A door opened and I could hear the twittering clearly now, a noise so continuous and unvaried in its high-pitched tone that it seemed electronic. I smelt something, acrid and sawdusty, and the smell got very strong. And then I saw them, like the opening shots in a thriller—thousands of white rats in cages from floor to ceiling down the length of a windowless room.

'Come along in,' the little man said. 'They won't bite!' He closed the door and we walked slowly down between the cages. There really were a great many rats, their paws testing the wire, nostrils aquiver, sampling the odorous delights of this stranger suddenly cast among them. I thought—what did I think? That the fiction had at last caught up with the reality and was about to overtake it? I did for a moment, and I longed for the director to shout 'cut!'

But nothing happened. 'This is the maze we've built for the rats,' the man said, showing me a labyrinth of little metal alley-ways and traps covered by a huge sheet of glass in the next room. 'We've proved it this way at least—the rats on Gerovital always find the cheese first.'

He demonstrated the experiment. And sure enough one rat got it and the other lost his way badly. It was like playing with trains. And it was a little like looking down on George Orwell's *Animal Farm*.

But the truth of the Balkans now is neither that of *The Lady Vanishes* nor *Animal Farm*. The first has truly vanished and the second hasn't yet—and I don't think will—become a reality. The truth, as usual, is more prosaic—and the maze, as always, is an appropriate symbol of it, the truth—in south-east Europe as elsewhere—is that there is some cheese at the end of the line and some rats are more equal than others.

PART FIVE

America

1

Return to America

[November 1972]

A few years ago it seemed as if everyone who could get the fare together and a roof in Europe was running from New York. It had become, so they said, Mug City—in every sense: you were a mug to live there; it was Fun City only for the muggers. It had become 'Ungovernable'—that was the fashionable word, with the high rise garbage on the sidewalks threatening to outdo the high rise buildings. In short, 'Old Manhattan, the Bronx and Staten' had taken a terrible tumble, while 'Mott Street in July' was a highway straight to the lower depths.

New York was the out place for most Americans—just as America in general was out for most Europeans, a continent which, in the years since Dallas, seemed to have forfeited all its claims as the Land of the Free. Thoreau's Walden pond had become a bloodbath: political assassination, black-white confrontation, police brutality, gigantic corruption, rioting, pollution—all topped off with sniper fire from book depositories and clock towers—this was the new American apple pie. And with it went the greatest horror of all, the murderous war in Viet Nam: hundreds of thousands, and eventually millions of Vietnamese maimed, massacred and made homeless: a holocaust the size of Hiroshima every few months. And all this for some long outdated cold war policy of 'containment', the 'Domino' theory, which even the CIA reported had no real validity in South-East Asia. The insane ghosts of Joe McCarthy and John Foster Dulles seemed to wield the real power when I lived there.

The great phrase of the late 'Sixties, which typifies the appalling American mood of the time, was, I suppose, General Le May's 'We'll bomb them back into the stone age.' Well, so much for the country which, for so long, for so many, had been the promised land. All the promises had been broken, and for quite a few Americans, and for others living there, it was time to pack up and go.

One of the people who left New York for London at the end of the decade was the great American writer and humorist, the 'peripatetic fabulist', S. J. Perelman. Another was myself. He had spent a lifetime there; I'd done only a few years' service. And without making any other comparisons our reasons for getting out seem to have been nearly the same. In Perelman's words New York had become 'Pestilential—the very air seems to have been re-breathed many times. London', he said, 'had a far more rational society than our own.' And I was very willing to agree with him. We must have knocked the dust off and set sail just about the same time.

And for several happy years he went his way—round the world in eighty days among other things—and I went mine, remembering New York and America, if at all, as a cauldron, a nightmare, and luxuriating in all the European virtues that had suddenly become sweet and sharp for me on my return: the civic order, the rational repose, the temperate airs.

I remember so well coming back to Europe, the first glimpse of the cool green land of Co. Cork from the boat deck, and later the berets—the smell of French tobacco on the quays of Le Havre, and finally the Southampton boat train moving through the tidy fields and back gardens, dripping and shining in that long shower which makes up an English summer. After the boiling heat and riots of our summers in New York, when from our apartment on Morningside Heights we looked across at the whole of Newark burning like Atlanta, this was the freshest sort of release imaginable. America had failed; Europe was the coming thing again. And Perelman and myself were going to be right in on it from the word go. The new Europe; an old and discredited America. That was the scenario.

And then last autumn came the blow: Perelman, I read, had gone back to live in New York. The clean air of London had quite palled. 'Their rye bread has no caraway seeds in it,' he said, 'and their salt beef doesn't compare with what you can get on the lower east side.' And no pastrami either. Well, what to do? This was a real slap in the face. The only thing to do was to go back there myself and check up on these American flavours, these virtues. Discover them indeed, for I'd not tasted them before. What was it that had taken Perelman back to New York? Something I'd obviously missed there myself—or something which my circumstances in that city had simply blinded me to? Scott Fitzgerald said that there were no second acts in the American experience. But perhaps that was too good a phrase to be true. I took a 'plane and went back there to find out.

For nearly two years I worked as an Information Officer in the United Nations Secretariat, high up in the glass-house looking out over the East river, one of the great views of the world. There was a Tannoy loudspeaker in my office and when I was tired of gazing at all the marvellous activity on the water, which was rarely, I could tune in to the various debates going on downstairs in the building—at the Security Council perhaps, or the General Assembly or in one of the committees, hearing over and over again an endless ritual of meaningless debate, careful phrases, stiff formalities—as far removed from the political realities as the mind and voice of diplomatic man could contrive. And my view of the river always underlined this division starkly —between man as he actually was and the UN's dry and isolated visions of him. It was as sharp and quick a thing as the physical act of swivelling round in my chair, away from the window, and turning on the box on my desk to hear the Foreign Minister of Ruritania lying through his teeth.

On certain fine spring days, or in the fall, to be high up in that building was to experience a stomach-lifting feeling of sensuous weightlessness, looking out on the sharp blaze—water, air and sky as crisp as broken ice—from a room silent and humming with warmth. One had the ridiculous sense of being in a magic machine, a personal airship. There was the sure feeling that one could detach the little glass cubicle from the rest of the building and float out over the Eerie and Pennsylvania railroad barges that swung awkwardly in the stream, saunter in the air above Welfare island before drifting down with a Circle Line steamer towards Chinatown and Battery Park. The activity on the river was so great that, though one could only sense this in the mass—in the steel cliffs slicing the water and the bulky tarpaulins of cargo turning on the current—one could imagine the human activity behind all this movement as sharply as if you were on the bridge of one of the tugs itself, ten feet away from the helmsman, feeling the first of the sea wind, hearing the wheel spin like a football rattle.

But in reality, three hundred feet up, through the sealed glass of my office, one felt nothing and all these pulsing mercantile inventions seemed devoid of man. From the UN building one was as conveniently distanced from the harsh human mechanics of the city as one was from those of the world.

Every so often people suggest other—as they see it—more appropriate uses for the UN building. I remember one British colour magazine saying, when I was there, how the conference areas would make a marvellous new international art centre while the imposing Secretariat building would readily adapt to the purpose of selling insurance. Well, one doesn't expect that international civil servants should work in hovels. But what does forcibly strike one about the UN building—as it might have done with the old League of Nations building or with some of the other UN agency buildings dotted about all over the world— is why do these splendid mountains bring forth so many mice? And if you work in any of these magnificent buildings for any length of time you will quickly come to an answer to that question. It is that in the UN one of the basic requirements is that the staff shall become mice. Servants of peace, yes—servants of many things. But essentially servants in a wrong and demeaning sense, called to serve only when required or allowed to do so by any one of the 136 nations who pay for, and therefore indirectly control, the UN and its agencies. So that to work there is to have not one boss but 136, any one of whom can breathe awkwardly down your neck, to say the least. This inevitably tends to paralyse corporate effort and promote great individual frustration. However, patience is a virtue, (it is the only real international currency) the financial rewards are reasonable—some would say over-generous—so that most staff swallow their initiatives, their frustrations, and get on with things as best they can. Through temperament I was unable to do this and my first problem when I went to America six years ago came in realizing that I was in the wrong job. And this had repercussions which soured my whole first experience of the country and its people. Here was a land—I could see it from my window looking at the tumultuous river view—visibly created through great initiative, intense individuality, founded on a charter whose essence was that of self-determination. And yet here was I locked away from it all, completely other-determined, sealed in a comfy office at the mercy of another charter whose essence would always be defined and redefined according to the political expediencies of more than a hundred distant governments. Far from being directly involved in the affairs of the world, as I had rather expected before joining the UN, I was expressly debarred from any meaningful involvement. We were International Civil Servants, which meant in practice that we were privileged but stateless citizens: rich refugees of the glass-house. From us there could be absolutely 'No comment'. And this was an awkward position to be in for someone who had spent most of his life commenting fairly strongly on something or other.

I remember once coming a cropper on a most innocent radio script of mine about wild-life conservation in East Africa. I had said something about elephant being more numerous in Tanzania than in Kenya. 'I don't think so,' a charming bureaucrat said to me. I said, 'Well, it's true.' 'Oh,' he went on, 'I'm sure it's true. It's just that you can't make that sort of comparison here. Have the Kenyans down our necks in no time.' 'Perhaps I could balance it then,' I said. 'I could say that Kenyan lions were fiercer than the ones in Tanzania.' 'Oh, my goodness no,' the fellow said, 'that would be compounding the damage.' And I could see the horrified thought in his eyes if this sort of thing were broadcast: an emergency meeting of the Security Council, battalions of lion and elephant massing on the Kenya–Tanzania border. To give voice to the very mildest opinion in the Secretariat building was considered as dangerous as a last ultimatum. To use the personal pronoun in a script, as I did in scripts several times, was to have Under-Secretaries turn to the East river wringing their hands, murmuring: 'The lights are going out all over the world.'

Why was the UN such a dull place to be in? Why was there so little love, so little urgency, so much desiccated vision? Why was an organization above all others dedicated to life and the living so empty of life itself?

In the years since Hammarskjöld's death, the Secretariat has come to hide behind a curtain whenever adverse criticisms are made of it. The principal mask is that the UN is only as good, as effective, as its member nations make it. Now politically, of course, there is a lot of truth in this. However, member nations are not responsible for running the Secretariat—for staff recruitment, for morale, for staff management, for the impetus and directions behind its day to day affairs. And the short answer here, I think, is that on this level the Secretariat has been disastrously managed over the years. A proper exercise in management-staff relations never seems to have been attempted. Apart from the security, secretarial and catering staff I should say hardly more than a score of people at the top have any meaningful work to do in the UN, or have any comprehensive grasp of what the Secretariat is, might or should be doing. The others, 1500 or so, mostly admirable and certainly dedicated men and women have to fiddle while the world burns.

It is true, of course, that the nature of the Secretariat's work does put a great strain on the staff's effectiveness. Apart from its reports and documents—the swords have been beaten into Xerox machines not ploughshares—there is no visible 'product'. There are very few moments when either success or failure can actually be held in the hand, clearly identified, praised or condemned; there is never a profit or loss account, the world keeps no such figures. It is an organization, almost by definition, without a true magnetic centre; it is geared either to the extremes of high drama or mind-bending boredom. It is not a rational entity; it has become the sum of our greatest but most unrealistic hopes and of our most unjustified disappointments. And we condemn it for both these excesses. It swings violently between illusion and frustration at the whims of its member states, and the citizens of those states. And the Secretariat, schizophrenically, swings with it. The task from the beginning should have been to stabilize the Secretariat in the middle ways of courage and commonsense, secure it more certainly against the caprices of its member states. Instead it has become a club where the management and staff have been beaten into submission so that those members can behave badly. The two sides are held together in an unholy alliance: we may never be black-balled; you will never be fired. It is empty of life because, of course, its member governments naturally prefer things that way, but just as much because it did not sustain life in itself when that opportunity existed in its earlier days.

Professional dissatisfaction discolours a new view more than anything else and I pretty soon came to dislike America and Americans as much as I disliked my job at the UN. I came to dislike the energy, confidence and vitality of the whole place, because—as I see now—I envied these qualities; they were no part of my job. Thus Americans became for me the sort of people I'd heard about years before—brash and pushy where they were not naïve and unlettered. I experienced all the old European warnings, the standard criticisms which we have been making about America from the beginning. And I thrived on it, mocking everything American, becoming a rampant hot-gospelling European myself, forever praising the old virtues of the old countries. With a boring dog-in-the-manger attitude I closed my eyes to the antics of the new world just as I did to inanities of the UN. Finally, along with Perelman and the others, we packed our bags and ran.

Well, when I got back from America this autumn I'm pleased to say I found that nearly all my hates had withered. I had ceased to mock. It was something of a conversion. It seems to me that many of our current thoughts about the country are out of true—about its violence, its political irresponsibility, its young people, its materialism, among other things. We seem to have got a lot of the present tone of the country wrong. Because the American horror of the past decade has been so prominently before us we have discounted much American virtue where we have not wilfully blinded ourselves to it. Proportionately, very few Europeans go to America for any length of time, yet the media gives us a quite disproportionate amount of information about the continent. And here is one of the main problems: we have come to know about the place through its great public issues at second-hand rather than through smaller local issues at first-hand. We tend to believe that because of this barrage of information, and because we share a common language, that Americans are less 'foreign', that we 'know' them. In fact as people they are as different from the English as any continental European is, and often more so.

Well, what did I find when I went back? What was the nature of the sea-change I underwent? There were many small things to start with, not great virtues but things which made life easier and less time wasting. We all know that, of course—the continent of the gadget, of the convenient in everything. We tend to forget that this can release people, especially women, for more useful pursuits. The domestic drudgery in America, over almost all the class spectrum, is considerably less than in Europe.

It is as simple as that. Food. Despite our ideas about its bland qualities, most popular American food—hot dogs, hamburgers, pastrami or pizza—has real flavour and, incidentally, a higher proportion of real meat. In fact that is one of the indelible marks of living there—the variety and flavour of its foodstuffs. One forgets that, as a continent, it draws for its sustenance on a climate as varied as the ethnic background of its cooks. Service in public places is a great deal more prompt and better natured. The reasons for this may be purely economic, I don't think they are—but, all right, if they are—you pay more for it but you get it, and quickly—a bargain I find soothing indeed. But these are details. What really attracted me to America this time was again something I'd derided before as the sage European: there is about the people something largely absent in Europe—a spirit of public self-inquiry; a willingness to subject their thoughts and behaviour to the open view, a need to consciously examine the dark areas, to test their traditions and personal assumptions empirically and continually.

Now this, in part, was always so. Experimentation, self-reliance, self-determination lie at the heart of the American experience. And in the long years of confidence no more was needed for the ideal community than these qualities of self be fostered positively for the general good. They were qualities largely directed to the problem of economic and physical survival. Now that those years are over, the frontiers all gone, now that there must be questions directed to a moral end, Americans ask them with an unparalleled fluency, approaching the matter of how to live with others and within themselves with the same attack that they once gave to mastering their outward environment. And this is where I found much of the excitement of the country—in this questioning of every intellectual frontier.

One may say that this present mood is no more than an enlargement of the old American addiction to 'patent cures' of every kind—be they medical, religious, political or psychological—just some of those old traditional, homespun 'parlour philosophies' now become epidemic. And this is true. This is largely what has happened. Europeans, of course, have often found this something of an embarrassment—these recurring American fads and fancies. Our mental and physical frontiers have been established so exactly and for so long that we do not often truly question them in public. We get by on any number of stiff upper lips. But the point is that our view of the current American passion for self-inquiry is not important. Americans are no longer interested in what we Europeans think of them. That chip on the shoulder about Paris fashions, London bobbys and the opera in Milan has almost totally disappeared. Americans have come to look inward; they have assumed an isolation just as, until quite recently, they assumed an overflowing expansionism. For better or worse they have become absorbed in themselves and the results of their deliberations should surely have messages for us if we can come to listen.

How should we live now? A question for all of us—and many people everywhere are asking it. But what makes America such a heady experience these days is that this proposal has become very much a public and not a private issue; it crackles in the air of widespread debate rather than in lone conversation: it has become something of communal more than individual importance. And coming from Europe into this almost tangible atmosphere of personal investigation I realized painfully my own long and comfortable acceptance of things as they were, my own lack of genuine inquiry. So this return journey turned out to be something of a release for me. There was, after all, a new world over there, a number of them in fact. Dr. Bill Welch, a New Yorker, ex-President of the American Heart Association and author of a very good recent autobiography, *What Happened In Between*, sums up the present climate very aptly I think.

'I think Americans have been both admired and criticized for their eternal examination of their interiors, of their inter-relationships, one with another: the quality of a marriage, the meaning of friendship, the ways in which to nurture and bring life to small children. It's overdone, to some extent—the "Inner" man, the "outer" man, the "company" man, the "organiza-tion" man, the "alienated" man, the "counter-culture" man—the number is legion. But at the same time it's a reflection of a kind of intensity that makes the electrical quality of America apparent when one moves, for example, from the relatively bland, fixed, serene, self-satisfied—if I may say so—attitude of the English. The serenity with which the European accepts his perfection is happily thrown into focus in the tentative, diffident, but searching attitude we are so criticized for. But it is just this quality of emotional generosity that is, so fresh, so engaging in certain American circles.'

James Dickey, poet and author of the novel and film *Deliverance*, takes the same line on this American generosity, though he has grave doubts about American self-inquiry.

'I think the best virtues of the Americans is their simplicity of response, the feeling of being generous towards a person— without a lot of self-questioning, without saying "Do I offer Joe Hone a beer because I feel guilty about Vietnam." It's the simplicity of response that's good about Americans, the un-complicatedness of it. But I do think that this continual tamper-ing with the human relationships by sociologists, and psychia-trists and so on is probably bad for people. The thing that I think is going wrong with us is this intensive self-questioning the very thing that you mention—the questioning of even the simplest motive: that you can't do simple things anymore. You've got to be consumed with metaphysical anxiety before you can eat an ice cream cone or a piece of pizza. That's what seems to be wrong with us if anything is.'

This may seem a more sensible attitude, but I don't think it's the more generally held one in America today. I spoke to Mrs. Stephanie Adleman, wife of a doctor at the University of Virginia, in Charlottesville:

'I think you're right about Americans. They do want to examine what they do. They want to know *why* they are doing it. I think there's a tremendous involvement in why we act the way we do. I know that I personally am fascinated about why I work the way I do, why I function the way I do. Why my children function. One of the things we found when we came back we found we had missed the most was this kind of discus-sion. And we were unable to have it with any Europeans. This whole comparison between America and Europe is very new to me. I don't think most Americans say "Now what are they doing in Europe?" America is very isolated. Americans live a very isolated kind of life. We're much more willing to expose ourselves to the public.'

Is it better not to tamper too much with the psyche—to guard one sense of self rather than to display it? Dr. Welch again:

'This is certainly a point of view. But it has been said—and I'm not sure that a better case can't be made out for it than not

—that the *un*-examined life is not worth living. Now this can exist, obviously, on more than one level; all of us can't be Henry James. But the more that one is in touch with the moment of one's life, the more one is aware of what's going on—you know, our life most of the time is such that we don't know what's going on until long after it's happened. And this really, at bottom, is a move in the direction of living now, living in the moment, and not dreaming our life away. It isn't an exaggeration, a philosopher's dream, to say that we spend our life without knowing how we spend it. It's wholly true that most of us, if we are honest about it, find that "my God, where has the time all gone to?" And I think it's in the direction of being more nearly *present* to our life that this contemporary mode is taking us. After all, the young people do find that there are many aspects of life that seem to them to be a waste of time, not worth the candle. And if it *is* worth the candle, no one is going to be worse off by having it severely questioned and, indeed tested by these inquiring young people.'

But James Dickey again sees it differently:

'I'm the great apostle of the anti-self-analysis movement which I hereby inaugurate this very minute! I've grown up in both regimes. And the people who came along while I was growing up, that is my mother and father, my relatives and so on, had relatively stable relationships with each other. You see—how infectious this thing is: I begin to talk in terms of the sociologist, in terms of "stable relationships" and all that. It's like—I remember what the fine poet and critic Randel Jarrell said about the relationship between poets and critics: critics are like people at a country fair who judge the pork contest—go up and prod the pig and say with a superior tone of voice to the pig: "Huh! What do you know about pork?"'

Of course, outside all this intellectual clamour about 'How to live now?' in America there remains for the visitor the corresponding physical clamour of the country, the tremendous impact of concrete, aluminium and glass, the endless natural and unnatural landscapes, mountains and freeways running away for ever: the huge scale of everything which is a slap in the face that you either get over or don't. When I lived there I didn't. All the 'poetry in concrete' business of New York, for example, left me pretty cold. If this was poetry then the language seemed to me peculiarly inhuman, icy and remote. Yet afterwards I felt vaguely that perhaps I'd missed something important in all this clamour and bigness, missed the point of it; the historical, social and architectural reasons behind it. So on this trip I thought I'd make up for it and lay myself open to one of the biggest and most clamorous cities anywhere—Chicago. Chicago, where the superlative is the norm, where everything and everyone has to go one better—the biggest and best and also the worst and the lowest, the great concrete mixer of America, ethnically and architecturally.

They call it the 'Windy City' for the almost permanent gale that buffets it from Lake Michigan lying to the north. But if the sun is out, as it was for the few days I was there, this wind becomes an exhilarating force, an airy tingling massage: arrogant hands which you feel at any moment will lift you off the sidewalk, Mary Poppins wise, and send you skimming up the sheer cliffs of concrete all about you. Many American cities, because of their huge verticals and long, flat, dead straight avenues, give you the feeling of vertigo from ground level; the sense in walking that you are just about floating and that if you began to run you'd simply take off. And Chicago particularly brings on this mood of imminent weightlessness. The City is like a huge kite, tied to the edge of the lake, straining and blowing and chattering in the wind, held by a last thread. One final gust, you feel, and the whole place will lift off and set sail for the clouds.

Chicago's buildings—particularly the fifteen-mile-long row of skyscrapers, towers and high rise apartments on Lake Shore drive—are the reason for this light-headedness. Chicago is the cradle and the home of the modern movement in architecture— The 'Chicago school' started by Louis Sullivan in the 1880s and afterwards developed by Frank Lloyd Wright, Mies van der Rohe and many others. It was an inspired collaboration between the mighty Chicago dollar and a group of equally adventurous architects and engineers. The buildings—for they were mostly stores, offices, warehouses and hotels—had to pay their way, make a profit: they had to work. This they did and more besides: they became a new definition of architecture and an art. Looking at them for the best part of a week, walking round the city with a handbook to these buildings, I began to appreciate the poetry in concrete as I had never done in New York. The whole point of the skyscraper, I realized, is that for architectural as much as financial reasons it should 'scrape the sky'. Louis Sullivan wrote nearly seventy years ago: 'The chief characteristic of the tall building is its loftiness. It must be tall, every inch of it tall. The force and power of altitude must be in it, the glory and pride of exaltation must be in it . . . It must be every inch a proud and soaring thing, rising in sheer exaltation, that from bottom to top is a unit without a single dissenting line.' Well, that's more or less exactly what Sullivan and his successors have contrived in Chicago. And the effervescence and variety of the buildings is quite startling. There is an extraordinary impudence in them; this is what strikes one most: how could they have come to be here, you ask?—surely not at the hands of any human agency. They are like Stonehenge in their gigantic mystery. To look up at the 1200-foot curving sides of the John Hancock center, or the same parabolic construction used in the First National Bank building, or the 700-foot shamrock-shaped Lake Point Tower apartments done throughout in bronze-tinted aluminium and glass, is to feel your hand shaking on the string of that kite, freed from the earth, just about to be carried up into the sky.

Chicago was an eye-opener for me. I'd expected rather a dismal, brutal place, a conglomeration of horror, gleaned second-hand over the years: the stockyards, with the blood seeping through into the rest of the city, violence as much legal as criminal, greed—a place where the rich have had their boots in the faces of the poor from the word go. And indeed there is still a lot of all this left in Chicago. Its ghettos lying behind the brilliance of Lake Shore drive—which Mayor Daley supposes do not exist—are equal to any in squalor and deprivation. At the same time Chicago is very much proof of the reality and continuity of the American adventure, even though it may be an appallingly unequal adventure for many. In its soaring buildings, its rampant human energy, its technical victories, its mastery of place and weather, there is even something of the American dream about it all. The overwhelming impression is of a city always straining at the boundaries of civic assumption, always pushing against traditional concepts, be they in society or in architecture, and often exploding through them—into violence but just as much into a new and extraordinary beauty. In Chicago one has to believe as much in the future success of the American adventure as one does in the present American horror. In a lot of American behaviour today one feels these two forces finely balanced against each other—their ability to renew the present and to corrupt it, to freshen the future or ruin it. This element of choice, a sense of equally realizable alternatives—be they moral or physical—is very strong in America. They seem all the time closer to radical decisions than most Europeans, and to be able to act on these choices much more readily and conclusively. Again, this seems very much part of their present self-inquiry: Americans are going out and looking for alternatives of any kind, giving themselves to, testing, many different kinds of living—in a word, making themselves *available*. This is particularly noticeable in their changing attitude to possessions, the new directions they are taking with their affluence, as Dr. Bill Welch underlined.

'It seems to me more and more in this country people have come to seek affluence not for possessions but for this special quality of mobility. They want to be able to move about; they want to be able to use, but they don't want to be burdened with ownership. Of course, there are still the highly exposed Americans who build yachts that would shame the *France*. But most Americans *lease* a yacht for a month and say the devil with it when the month is up. They're not burdened with the laundry of the captain and the salaries of the crew. And so it is with houses, mink coats, with places in the country, with flats in town: what they really want to do is put their hands in their pockets and whistle themselves on board a transatlantic plane with no luggage and when they arrive they have what they need and they drop it there. They turn round and come back. They move with the sense of freedom that certainly never attended the affluent of other generations who moved in two or three flat cars when they went from their summer place to their winter place or their town house to their country house. There has been very much a tendency to turn to more enduring values, to drop the evidence of conspicuous consumption, and perhaps, just perhaps, this means that the outer life will be less elaborate and the inner life richer.'

Is Affluent America dispossessing itself? Not quite, I should say, but there is no doubt they appear to be following the young in their taste for the unencumbered life.

Young America: how much we've heard about them—and how much of that seemed to me irrelevant when I got there again. The drug scene, the hippies, frenzied music, strobe lights —the whole desperately weary bag of tricks that was thrown at us all through the 'Sixties. No doubt a lot of it was true— for a few people. But the media men got onto it and had us believe that every American under twenty-five lived on Haight-Ashbury, bedecked in beads and flowers and stoned out of his mind.

What struck me in the two campuses I visited, at Ann Arbor in the north and the University of Virginia in Charlottesville, was the maturity and balance of most of the students. One missed particularly the polarization so often found among the English young—between a narrow academic seriousness and a juvenile, know-all flippancy. Certainly there were those American students who approached their work in too narrow a manner —and those who did little more than throw footballs about all the time. But even these groups found time to ask as many questions outside their discipline as inside it. Again, it was how to live now as much as how to interpret mediaeval acrostic poetry. And, as Dr. Welch pointed out to me, for quite a few American students this living properly was more important to them than their work:

'I think the young Yale boys that are carpenters, entrepreneurs of the apartments of New York—they're pretty happy kids. They're learning perhaps nothing more than to be carpenters, they may never be cabinet makers, but in the meantime they're not torn apart by all the agony of being in a highly structured corporation: they don't go in stiff collars to a bank every day. They use their hands, their heads, they see people and from their point of view they're leading a rich and rewarding life. It's been a matter of very great interest to me to discover—not to have it announced to me, but to discover—that any number of young people who may be living in what used to be called sin, live very serene domestic lives with one another, without any of the external commitments that ordinarily attended such arrangements. I know any number of young men who have had elaborate educations and what do they do? They open a carpenter's shop in the village, they take on electrical repair jobs, they open lamp shops, they move to farms.'

Thomas Jefferson's University of Virginia in Charlottesville, opened in 1825, I think is one of the great sights of America. In the success of its total concept, of architecture linked with learning, it seemed to me unequalled by any university elsewhere. Jefferson's idea from the beginning was to create an academic village rather than just one or a succession of large buildings, so that here the students are housed in four long lines of individual single-storey rooms giving out onto a central lawn, descending in terraces with trees and paths. There are ten, two-storied Palladian pavilions, no two alike, situated at intervals along these student lines and originally the professors lived upstairs and gave their lectures on the ground floor. The lines are fronted throughout their length by a white-columned porch, a covered way, so that students, teachers and the various schools were absolutely integrated while yet never being on top of each other. At the northern end of the grass rectangle lies the focal point of the whole scheme: a magnificent rotunda building. The concept is Palladian, the classic revival of Greece and Rome—colonnades, arcades, doric columns and so on. But Jefferson was an American, a romantic classicist, and he has interpreted these European forms in a uniquely American manner: in the local very red brick, white-painted wood everywhere and stucco. The effects are marvellously delicate, precise: the brilliant primary colour, the white trim, the serenity, the human scale of the long colonnades, the climax of the rotunda. It is pre-eminently a village, an unforced, undaunting place to live and learn: space, grace and absolutely no pace.

It was late afternoon in the fall when I was there, but in Virginia that's as warm as an English summer, so that the students were still grilling up things on little portable barbecues outside their doorways. Others sat on the grass beneath the huge trees—planted, though of course never seen by Jefferson. The university orchestra wavered about uncertainly with a symphony from some building behind me; the meat began to burn on the charcoal, singeing the air with odd savoury breaths, and students carried logs in for their fireplaces. Their rooms were very simple: white-washed walls, two small windows, a double wooden latticed door, colourful bedspreads and posters, fires beginning to crackle, gallon jars of Californian burgundy, a lot of paperbacks, a few guitars.

Well, there was certainly a long continuity of civilized reason about the place. And this was very much Jefferson's ideal: the academic village, yet with privacy. The virtue of good, simple things—in brick and landscape, music and food and drink, and living at one with everything. And here it all was. In many ways his university was the first of the young communes in America and his ideals seem paralleled to a remarkable extent by the American young today: getting out of the big city rat race, as Jefferson did by returning to Monticello, the remarkable house he built for himself on the hills above the university in Charlottesville; making good locally with your own hands and ideas, as Jefferson did with the many extraordinary technical innovations he brought to the construction of his house—designing his own furniture, wall-paper, curtains, a unique bed that gives onto both bedroom and study, automatic swing doors, a variety of dumb waiters, an immense calendar clock whose strange mechanics arch right over the hall door and down into the basement—allowing his own specially inventive genius full play among all the blue prints of an old, yet valued civilization; inquiring into all given values, reinterpreting them. Well, this is very much the direction of the American young today.

Travelling five hundred miles south, from Charlottesville, Virginia, to Columbia, South Carolina, is to move from the American age of reason to the more present America of unorganized dream and sensation. The sharp variations, in climate and geography, of the first colony disappear completely—replaced by a flat and burning landscape. Here one finds all the unnerving decor of urban America—freeways and bill-boards and motels and all the other nothing buildings trembling vacantly in the haze, carrying on for ever into a dirty horizon. Driving the fifteen miles from the airport to Columbia it was impossible to tell where the airport ended and the city began; impossible to define the city at all, to mark the suburbs or the downtown area, and the sun too harsh to take a bearing on so that direction was lost and one seemed to be floating in the open car, rising up and down on the gently lapping folds of tarmac: the deep south, like an ocean, not a land at all. Here was another America altogether: an America free of the past completely, where one felt anything went, where anything could happen.

James Dickey is poet-in-residence at the University of South Carolina and his house is on the edge of a warm artificial lake the far side of town. There's a ping-pong table permanently on the terrace, a jetty with a small speedboat, trees everywhere, flowers, gardeners padding quietly about the place. I swam out to an island in the middle of the lake and watched the strong light tilt everywhere around me, silhouetting the grand mansions round the edge. Then I eased my way back through the carpet of liquid gunmetal, back to the jetty where we had whisky in heavy tumblers, the malt smell, a slight Scottish sweetness, mixing with the slightly sour airs of clay rising from the lake now that the heat was over and it was evening. First, the dunlopillo of the freeways, now this beautifully contrived arcadia round the lake, the earth tamed and watered, nature at our disposal.

But James Dickey's best-selling novel and film *Deliverance* tells a very different story indeed—four townsmen on a week-end's canoeing in the wilds of North Georgia whose attempts to enjoy the natural world by taming it end in a violent human and natural disaster. His title, *Deliverance,* is two-edged at the very least: nature, particularly American nature, will just as surely deliver you into evil as from it. 'Them thar hills' spell murder more than gold. It is a perennial American theme—the violence which seems always to accompany those who pursue the American dream, which always catches up with them in the end, and delivers them, if not to death, then back into their ordinary nightmares. Violence—the main ingredient, some say, of the American apple pie. James Dickey had few doubts about this.

'In America what we are most terrified by in our time is being set upon, by malicious strangers: by gunmen in the street, muggers, hold-up men. It doesn't matter whether this occurs way off in the backwoods of the Georgia mountains. It's all the same feeling: we're terrified—of someone stepping up to us— someone who doesn't care anything about our life, who had just as soon shoot you as look at you. In fact some of them would *rather*. What I wanted to do in *Deliverance* was to say something about what one *does* in a situation where one is beset by malicious strangers. I had the setting way off in the woods where there could be no police called or where no agency of the state could possibly intervene. It has to be done by the people involved. We've had centuries of injustice in this country—injustice towards the black, towards the Indian, towards various minority groups. What frightens me is when I step out of a hotel in New York and see a crowd of blacks coming toward me down the street is that here might conceivably be people who would consider doing me in and robbing me of the few dollars' change in my pockets—who might consider this action perfectly justified because of several centuries of injustice which has been visited upon them by white people—ancestors of mine, or at least white men—and actions in which I had no part at all.'

This fear of violence is, indeed, very widespread in America. And there is good reason for it: people *are* bumped about a lot, to say the least. On the other hand it seemed to me, and to several Americans I spoke to, that some of the bumping, at least, is exaggerated. And something else has happened too: this climate of fear, induced by the media and by a highly infectious group hysteria, has come to *create* a lot of the violence. And this is especially so in the rich and nervous ghettos of New York.

L. J. Davis is a novelist and journalist with various New York magazines and lives in Brooklyn where he does a column for the local newspaper. Very much in the Runyon tradition, New York is not just his oyster: it's a dozen oysters, all of them pearl-filled, and he takes them on with hungry relish. With him many of the fearsome myths of the city dispersed. He has an appetite for the place, not a fear. It makes all the difference.

'My wife is a social worker who goes to the worst neighbourhoods in the city as a matter of course. Nothing has ever happened to us. I've never even witnessed a street crime. Once I saw an old man fall over dead but that wasn't a crime. No, it's bizarre to think that I as a parent and husband would raise my family in such a place, as myth would have it, exists in New York City. This is a myth, a preposterous myth. And yet one that feeds on itself. If you *act* as though downtown Manhattan or Brooklyn is a war zone, if you act as though you were going to be mugged, you are creating a self-fulfilling fantasy. You create this myth and no one goes there. The place eventually becomes wide open. And the people that you have created in your fantasy as your potential oppressors and attackers of course will participate in the myth with you. Jolly good, of course they will.'

I put it to Davis that you could walk round ghettos or ethnic areas in a city anywhere else in the world without *automatically* getting mugged because you were white. And this brings us to the black-white confrontation in America, an area where there has been little, if any real progress, and no grounds for future optimism.

'Well, bear in mind this, that New York has seen in the last decade a large influx of desperately poor blacks from the south. They come from a society where they were oppressed by whites —in the most vicious, heartless, sadistic manner possible—for 300 years. They have now moved north into a more libertarian society, but bearing these attitudes—the seething hatreds, that is endemic in the culture—naturally, if you are oppressed for 300 years by a bunch of white slobs you are going to hate whites like nobody's business. What we are seeing now is a great breaking out, a boiling over, of this rage against the nearest victims, against the whites, as it happens. At the same time the whites in the city, panicking as they are, have created a scenario for the blacks to follow: the whites have almost literally set themselves up as victims—by exaggerating the amount of crime far beyond reality and behaving like victims: you see a man coming down the street, say you are black, you are enraged against whites, you're 14, 15, 16—you've got a bunch of friends you want to show off for—you see a guy coming down the street and he looks at you, with a mixture of fear, which has been built up, in him—you know, his eyes begin to skitter, to go back and forth— why, you've got a victim man! What fun it would be to rip him off. Why the guy's scared of us. Fantastic! I mean, you can see how the scenario feeds on itself.'

You certainly can: New York is a place to keep your eyes open, your wits about you. But if you do this and manage not to become an actor in that violent scenario it remains not only an exciting place to visit but also to live in. Certainly New York is totally unsympathetic towards necessary communal or familial life, totally undomestic, often violent, uncomfortable, dirty. On the other hand we should give it credit for what it *is*: a great creator and satisfier of *individual* life, a city of the ego, a very expensive educational game, a toy not like other toys. It creates the thirsts it slakes at the expense of all sorts of proper foods: a big concrete cylinder of pure oxygen: it has its uses just as much its abuses. And in enjoying it or understanding it almost everything depends on whether we approach it with fear or favour. If we are disappointed we should not always blame the city; we may simply have been playing a role in one of its many unpleasant scenarios, rather than living its often marvellous reality. New York seems to me in this way—in these ordinary times where the air is thin with pedantry, fear, pessimism, compromise—to be, for all its disadvantages, a very necessary city: the place to go for a fix, which can become a cure and not an addiction.

A lot of my American experience had that effect on me—the effect of a release from many old and ill-considered assumptions, about myself, about Europe, above all about America. The public horrors of the last decade have blotted out for us, and for many Americans, much of the virtue of the country. And indeed these last ten years seem to me to have been the worst ever in the American experience. Nor can one say that they are out of it yet, not at all. What one can say is that there is in America, as well as the horror, a similarly unequalled ability to inquire into their malaise and an ability—in terms of personal, if not yet political effort—to rid themselves of it. As in its earlier history it has become again a continent of many experiments—political, social, above all personal. Just as Thoreau did when he left the town of Concord for Walden pond, Americans have turned back on themselves. Thoreau questioned the sum of all American values in his time and sought to define his own, living by himself in the woods for two years—and that is America now. Thomas Jefferson did much the same thing in building Monticello and returning there for an extraordinarily exuberant and inventive life. And these qualities are far more a part of the American scene today than any of the horrors.